At Christmas
the Heart
Goes Home

A
HOLIDAY
TREASURY BY
MARJORIE HOLMES

DOUBLEDAY

NEW YORK

LONDON

TORONTO

SYDNEY

AUCKLAND

At Christmas the Heart Goes Home

PUBLISHED BY DOUBLEDAY
a division of Bantam Doubleday Dell
Publishing Group, Inc.
666 Fifth Avenue, New York, New York 10103

DOUBLEDAY and the portrayal of an anchor with a
dolphin are trademarks of Doubleday, a division of
Bantam Doubleday Dell Publishing Group, Inc.

DESIGNED BY ANNE LING

Library of Congress Cataloging-in-Publication Data
Holmes, Marjorie
[Selections.   1991]
At christmas the heart goes home : a holiday treasury /
by Marjorie Holmes.—1st ed.
p.   cm.
A collection of stories, poems, and prayers originally
written by the author.
1. Christmas—Literary collections.   I. Title.
PS3515.04457A6   1991
818'.5409—dc20   91-8418
                                                                        CIP

ISBN 0-385-41292-4

Acknowledgments

Grateful acknowledgment is made to the editors of the following publications, where many of these prayers, poems, and articles first appeared:

"Evergreens, the Color of Christmas," "Christmas Stars," "Whimsical Sights and Sounds," "The Mystery and Magic of Christmas," "His Very Own Card," "Gifts Are for Loving—and *Using*," "Shopping Spree, Small Boy," "What Becomes of Dolls?" "Share Your Christmas Party," "The Gift That Multiplied," "Let It Be a Merry Christmas for Everyone in the World," " 'Merry Christmas, Mrs.

Contents

CHAPTER 4
Christmas, a Time for Caring   103

Foreword

WELCOME TO
MY CHRISTMAS!

For years I've wished I could have a huge Christmas party for all my friends. Especially the people who read my books and articles and stories, and who followed my columns in *Woman's Day* and the Washington, D.C., *Evening Star* for so long. My files bulge with their wonderful letters (the best gift a writer can have). I came to know many of them in person, some became my closest friends. But whether we met or not, there was a bond between us.

Warm and shining, flooding the heart sometimes. Especially at Christmas. If only I had a house as big as my dream and could fling open the doors to welcome everybody in.

So when Doubleday suggested a treasury of my Christmas writings, I rejoiced. It seemed somehow a way to fulfill that dream.

Like most people, Christmas has always been my favorite holiday. Its enchantment begins in childhood and casts a spell that never ends. As a young wife and mother beginning her career as a writer, I found it a source of inspiration I could not resist. I wrote about Christmas for a dozen magazines, and later was so profoundly moved one Christmas Eve, I knew I simply had to write a novel about the Nativity, told as the love story of Mary and Joseph.

But the richest source of Christmas material was my biweekly column, *Love and Laughter,* which appeared in the *Star* for almost twenty-five years. With the help of my son I went through all these writings, typing and photocopying Christmas. Winnowing and gleaning; stories and sketches and sometimes readers' letters and poems. What memories the job brought back, what a joyful sharing. And as we worked, it seemed as if the fantasy of

that huge Christmas celebration party were
about to come true. Why, there was plenty of
room! Hurry up and get ready. Old friends
would be arriving. And new ones opening the
door. It's wide open to everybody, I began to
think . . . and say it now:

*If you love Christmas, come on in! Welcome
to my party. Consider this is your invitation.*

As you open this book, please imagine it
as our front door with a big wreath on it, and
sprigs of mistletoe over every sill inside. The
lights of the Christmas tree are sparkling. People are already gathered around it, some of
them singing carols. Others are laughing and
talking beside a crackling fire. Neighbors and
friends, grandparents and children: teenagers
and small fry, kids home from college. Come
in, come in to join us. Bring your family, bring
your friends; the more the merrier!

The coffeepot is steaming, hot and fragrant. There is a big bowl of punch and plenty
of cookies. Also a table laden with a lot of
other good stuff. Help yourself.

I'll show you through the house if you
like, there's plenty of time. We'll even sit down
together someplace where it's quiet, and exchange the best gifts of all, our personal stories.
Mine are already here, waiting to be opened

and read. And my heart is waiting for yours. But somehow I feel I already know them, just as you will probably recognize yourself in mine. Your own family and holiday customs, your own memories echoing . . . echoing.

The magic of Christmas makes all this possible. The Christmas Spirit floods our hearts and makes us one. So welcome to my Christmas! Let's celebrate together. As Tiny Tim would say, "God bless us, every one!"

Part 1

Expectation

Chapter 1

THE MOST BEAUTIFUL
TIME OF THE YEAR

Mothers Keep All These Things

Christmas is a time when mothers feel close to Mary. And the presence of that young girl–mother always seems especially close on the day we make the annual pilgrimage to the attic to bring down the family decorations—those familiar if somewhat bedraggled banners that seem to symbolize the true arrival of the season. No matter where they're stored, not until a woman has searched them out and sorted them over does it seem possible that the calendar isn't kidding. . . . Christmas is truly upon us and it's time to cope with it.

What in the world did people do in the days before attics and closets and basements? Attics with their clutter!

As you grope around for the light switch, that clutter springs into view. You regard it with a kind of affectionate hopelessness for an instant, then head for the corner given over to Christmas accumulations. The bags, the boxes, the cartons spilling over. Where in the world does it all come from, and why do you keep it, anyway?

And suddenly, quite clearly out of the Christmas story, a shining phrase speaks to you: *Mary kept all these things and pondered them in her heart.*

Mary kept all these things . . . Musing on the curiously significant words, you kneel in your slacks and sweater, and begin the enormous task of disentangling ropes of tinsel and taking inventory. The tinsel is getting a trifle tarnished, but maybe it'll do just one more year. The heavy wads of icicles thriftily rescued at how many last minutes from how many drooping trees. The fragile, colored balls—so many shattered; yet, remarkably, some of these delicate ornaments date back to your first year of marriage.

You give an amused jangle to the sleigh bells that once sang from a bobsled belonging to your grandfather. Hold up the giant red stocking that the children love to stuff with toys and hang beneath a spray of pine or holly on the door. Faded now, the seams beginning to split. Dye it? Mend it? Or throw it out and buy one of those big fancy felt ones trimmed in fur and sequins?

You unwrap the faithful figures for the crèche. Baby Jesus and his tiny cradle. Mary, Joseph. The shepherds, the Wise Men. The sheep are getting rather grubby, and one of the camels has lost an ear.

Really, you should throw out so many things. Take the stable. The boys wanted to make it themselves, so you let them, and didn't have the heart to tell them the roof was crooked. (Its defects could always be disguised with straw.) And the angel was always too big for the scene. An awkward plaster angel molded and painted with watercolors by your little girl in second grade. She'd never miss it, she's in junior high now. Resolutely you drop it in the wastebasket. But suddenly, with the same compulsion that makes you rush back to the fireplace to rescue their notes or cards or drawings, you reach to the bottom of the basket and haul it forth again. You just can't do it. Because—though its creator would never miss her lumpy angel—you would.

Mary kept all these things . . . Mothers keep all these things.

You look about. Everywhere is mute testimony to the countless things a mother clings to: a baby carriage, a high chair, a crib. Oh, but there is justification for these, you hasten to assure yourself. One day there will be grandchildren coming to visit, or others to lend them to. These are useful things.

But what of all the rest? Those cartons filled with battered little first books and stub-toed shoes? The mountainous stacks of scrapbooks bursting with snapshots? The souvenirs? That football helmet dangling from a nail. A Cub Scout suit, a daughter's first prom dress. Such . . . foolish things.

"Clear out" we are told repeatedly by the efficient ones. Live modern, streamline, cut down. Or think of the needy; give things away. And ruthlessly, over and over, you do. And yet a woman, too, suffers from a very real and peculiar need. A hunger of the heart that can be appeased only by these small items that would be utterly useless and meaningless to anyone else. And it relates us to our mothers and their mothers before them.

KEEPSAKES is written on a large box on the shelf. And in it, fondly labeled by fingers long still, is a yellowed sailor suit that belonged to my husband as a little boy; a ribbon-tied packet of his own first laboriously lettered Christmas cards; and a worn pair of small red boots. His mother, too, kept all those things.

When we were first married I used to wonder why. And what was I supposed to do with them? Then I had a child, and I understood. I also wanted to clutch, to hold, to keep every possible moment of this marvelous experience. When our baby's hospital identification bracelet was lost I felt bereft. Faced with our first move and the absolute necessity of getting rid of many mementos, I suffered—and in the end weakened and threw out the pans instead. And when our daughter clumped around proudly in the red boots that her dad had adored at five, or slept in the selfsame cradle, or had her photograph taken in his clothes, it did something strange to me. It was like glimpsing him from the beginning; it helped me to see him whole.

And it gave me a sense of continuity. Of

something eternal. Of clasping hands with an endless procession of women who had gone before me, and of reaching out to join hands with those to come.

Mothers keep all these things. Because they are the physical reminders of our children, the shed garments of a time that, however hectic it may be now, will, we instinctively sense, someday seem precious.

Mary kept all these things and pondered them in her heart . . .

Yet there is another kind of keeping that goes beyond even these symbols. Even if we live in small apartments where there is no space for extras, how many things a woman keeps through sheer "pondering in her heart."

"That's what a mother does all her life, really," a friend once said. "At first, as you go about your meals or the housework, it's mostly active thinking—about their health or their grades or their playmates and whether or not you can afford something they need or want. And the problems get bigger and more complicated as the children grow older. But after a while it isn't so much the problems you ponder as it is the memories. Often memories of very little things, but things you will always hold dear."

This is true. The mind becomes a teeming treasure house, so full it sometimes spills over to furnish those family anecdotes we tell to friends and relatives, or sometimes pass along for generations: "Grandma always told this story about spanking the wrong boy. All the kids were lined up on the porch and they looked so much alike in their overalls and straw hats that she grabbed one, thinking it was Uncle Frank—" . . . "You were about four when this happened, Nancy—you always slept with this teddy bear, and one night—"

Mary kept all these things and pondered them . . .

You feel a renewed kinship for Mary, sitting there on the attic floor among the flotsam and jetsam of living. You gaze at the tiny Christ Child curled asleep in his rude little manger. What were some of the things his girl-mother pondered? You wonder. What secret thoughts?

I remember the night he was born. The stable was quite cold but the hay smelled sweet and his cry was the most thrilling sound I had ever heard . . .

I remember the journey into Egypt. We were in a hurry and very frightened, but he slept all the way, he was good as gold . . .

And what reminders of his childhood did Mary, like most mothers, save? His first little garments, or the sandals in which he learned to walk? A wooden toy cart, perhaps, that his father had made for him?

And did she visit perhaps with other women, drawing water at the well? *"I think the worst problem we ever had was when we lost him, coming home from Jerusalem. We were nearly frantic until we found him in the Temple . . ."*

You rise from the floor and take up a bulging box. Again this year, as usual, its contents will all make the journey into the holiday with the family. The lumpy angel will beam once more above the homemade stable. The battered bells will sing out their merry music each time people dash through the door. The beloved red family stocking, mended and refurbished with a bright bow, but still the same, will dangle beneath branches of pine, and from it will jut a doll with one arm missing, a dented bugle, an enormous candy cane. Simply because that's the way the children want them. It wouldn't be Christmas otherwise.

Because Christmas is for keeps. It comes every year and will go on forever. And along with Christmas belong the keepsakes and the customs. Those humble, everyday things that a mother clings to, and ponders, like Mary, in the secret spaces of her heart.

Evergreens, the Color of Christmas

How grateful we should be for evergreens. For the spruces, the firs, the cedars, the pines. All the varieties of trees that refuse to give way to winter, and however bleak the day rest our eyes and restore our spirits with their banners of green.

The sky may be steely gray; yet against it toss the green plumes of the pines. Tall and straight they stand, these "first families" of the trees, an ancient race we are told, dating back to the beginnings of man.

Cone-clotted, the spruces sweep the ground. The blue spruce most nearly reflect the cool colors of winter, for their crisp pointy needles range from blue-green to silvery white. Yet they, too, lend their lovely green. The firs hold their ripe cones proudly erect, like offerings from their ferny hands. The balsam firs lend their fragrance as well; their sap congeals in perfumed beads; their needles fill pillows that are sweet for sleeping.

Whatever their nature or species, the evergreens help us to hold fast to the hue so vital to our eyes. For green is the color of summer and life when the world is awake and stirring;

the color of leaves and vines and grass when the skies are blue and the sun shines warm. "See, see," the evergreens proclaim, "life is not over, only resting, all is not frozen and stripped. Summer will come again and all the greens return. Meanwhile, take comfort in us, look at us and remember some things are eternal." Yes, green is the color of promise and faith.

Green is also the color of Christmas. For it is the prickly living boughs of the evergreens that we carry inside to celebrate. They make our mantels festive, their wreaths adorn our doors. And though some people may find it necessary to substitute artificial trees, no substitute of plastic or silver can duplicate the wonder of a Christmas tree of genuine vibrant green. A tree cut and brought fresh from the forest to stand as a symbol of life—all life. The tender new life of the Christ Child—or any child, in the cradle. We can almost hear the tree breathing, speaking to us in little friendly whisperings in the night. And when we come in from the cold and sniff its sweet tang, we feel refreshed and joyous.

How grateful we can be. When the rest of the world is resting, stripped and bare and bleak, how lucky we are to have these faithful beauties. How good of God to give us ever-greens.

Attaboy, God!

Evening, and a light snow beginning to fall . . . The children press their noses excitedly to the window, urging the frail flakes on.

The snowflakes are tentative, only a pale glinting in the kitchen light. Like fireflies darting, or lost spirits seeking a way to go. A few settle, cling to a twig or lightly dust the ground.

"Will there be enough for a snowman? Can we go sledding tomorrow?"

"I doubt it. Come on now, bedtime."

You lead them reluctantly toward baths. By the time the commotion of hurled towels and missing pajamas and who gets which story is settled, they've forgotten. . . . Except for the four-year-old. Piling out of bed, he darts to the window, struggles back the curtains, and emits a joyful shout.

"It's snowing, it's really snowing! *Attaboy, God!*"

The fervor, the joy, the awe. The sheer

exultation, bringing others spilling from their nests to gaze upon this wonder, the now swiftly falling snow. This white explosion, this whirling, sparkling stardust that will change their world by morning. What a marvel. . . . And surely no prayer of praise and thanksgiving was ever uttered with more enthusiasm than that simple outburst.

God is so close to children, so real, if you simply provide the name for that which they instinctively feel. Fresh from their own Creator, they sense his closeness in a way more intensely pure and certain than it will ever be again.

Attaboy, God!

Dignified? No. But such genuine joy, such fervent praise. Such absolute acceptance of the nature of God and his power to bestow.

We are so wordy, we adults. We make our Creator so complex. We need to become again like little children shouting our welcome to wonders almost too marvelous to believe. A flower that grows and bursts from a tiny seed. Whirling snow. This magical world and our lives upon it. How incredible, how glorious!

We ought to leap from our sluggish beds and rush to the windows of life, rejoicing. Applauding. Praising. Calling out with every cell of our beings: "Attaboy, God!"

Beauty in Your Own Backyard

The brilliant colors of Christmas that begin to blaze at dusk. Whole neighborhoods, so ordinary, taken for granted, suddenly assume a gay and profligate identity of light. Rooftops are rimmed with rubies, doorways are diamond-decked. No sultan's palace could surpass their splendor that spills even on to the shrubs and hedges and trees in the yard; such gaudy necklaces, such garlands of brilliance—all clamoring "Look at me!" Were these ever simply familiar houses and yards? Will they ever be again? No matter—for now, right now, you live in Fairyland!

The Small Fry Say

Mother, at dinner table: "You'd better get your letter off to Santa or he won't know you want that big red fire engine."

Six-year-old, grinning at his father: "If he doesn't he's pretty dumb, he's sitting right here."

This Is the Busy Season

This is the busy season. The time of delightful yet also frenzied preparation—cards to be written and mailed, fruitcakes to be wrapped, the packages we meant to have out of the way by now, the decorations that you hoped to make as special as a magazine picture this year.

But of far more importance, actually, are those events which mean so much to the children. That concert the junior choir is giving, their parties and programs at church and school.

And if it should come to a choice between the preparations and the programs, let the preparations go.

What people on your card list mean as much as your own youngsters? How can the finest gifts, the most elegant decorations, compare to the face of your boy or girl as they march into the auditorium and eagerly scan the audience for you?

Or the light of relief and joy when they spy you and shyly wave to you?

The Christmas Greens

"May we go? Please may we go to the Christmas Greens Show?" the children clamor. "It's free!"

"Free?" Your husband looks up from his checkbook. "That's the best news I've heard this time of year—let's go!"

"The tree for the birds, that's what I want to see," the littlest declares as you all pile into the car.

"Aaah, that's for the birds," a brother says scornfully. "What I wanta know is will they have the cookie tree?"

"Well, dears, they usually do," you remind them. "But there'll be lots of other things anyway."

You join the throng of parents and children heading for the vast glass house that sparkles like ice in the sun.

The Botanical Gardens, usually smelling

so damply tropical, have an exhilarating new aroma. A tang of fir trees, a pungent spicing that seems brewed of all Christmases past, assailing your senses, stirring up memories. Yet heralding with a sudden sharp excitement the present holidays.

As for lots of other things? Beauty is here in such bounty one feels like a child on Christmas morning; it is almost too much to comprehend. Then you must begin: A forest of Christmas trees flaunt their fairy lights, each gemmed and adorned as if to outdo the others, like ladies dressed for a ball. While tiny mimics of these taller sisters twinkle with a glory of their own, table-size.

"And look, *Mantels and Hearths of Different Nations*—" Slowly you move from one to another, marveling. Scrambling in your bag for pad and pencil, you make swift sketches, scribble notes. "That Swedish hanging, did you ever see anything more enchanting? Or the Swiss!" . . . "You know, those swags are a good idea, and they don't look too hard to make." Everywhere other voices are exclaiming, comparing, contemplating. "See how cleverly they've used pine cones and gilded pods—"

How cleverly. With what loving inventiveness. Spurred only by the spirit of Christmas, and the sheer joy of fashioning beautiful things.

For there are no prizes for these exhibits, no competitions. Nothing but the sheer delight of sharing their handiwork with others who may also be inspired to make something more of Christmas than merely shopping in a store. For these reasons alone, dedicated women have labored to bring this about, and you think of them with gratefulness.

Here, at least, is one answer to the commercialism rampant elsewhere. . . .

The wreath-trimmed windows. The gaily decked doors. The tables lavishly spread for Christmas dinner as celebrated from the bayous of the South to the rock-bound New England coast.

"Yes, honey, in a minute," you keep telling the small fry tugging at your coat as you try to take in them all.

Then you are finally joining them to marvel at *Toy Land,* where Santa's own elves must have furnished the eight enchanting rooms.

Then on to see Baby Jesus and all the angels acting out the traditional Christmas carols. And finally *Holiday Sharing,* where baskets bulge for the needy, and here, too, each is a finely wrought thing.

You leave at last, as after some joyous feast. Filled to the brim with it, the sight and the smell and the song of it—and the ideas it has engendered dancing like the mobiles in your head.

Moments That Make You Proud

When a little girl can't get past the Salvation Army kettles without dropping in coins until her allowance is all gone.

The Small Fry Say

Five-year-old before the television: "Santa Claus sounds like he's got a cold." Worriedly, "Maybe he caught it from me! Because if he's the spirit of love like you say," she reasons, "he could be everywhere and get my germs."

Christmas Stars

On the way home from church the littlest one presses her nose against the glass. "Jesus had to be born at Christmas," she announces. "Because there's more stars then."

"Not more stars," corrects a brother as they pile out of the car. "There's always the same number of stars, isn't there, Mother? And they didn't even *name* it Christmas till after he was born."

"All right, winter." She slides happily along the jeweled walk. "There had to be lots more stars so the shepherds could see them."

"I just *told* you—there couldn't be any more stars. Maybe it just seems like it because in winter the stars seem brighter."

"Why? Do stars like cold weather? Is that why they light up their fires more and sparkle better?"

"I give up." With a playful spank he turns her over to you and plunges on into the house.

You take her mittened hand and stand for a moment, sharing her fascination with the sky. It is like a vast meadow tonight, strewn with a million star daisies. And roses carved from sapphires. And silver cockleburs. A few get tangled and lost in shifting white thickets of clouds, and a few have dipped so close they seem caught in the fingers of the trees. They flash enticingly there, almost close enough to pluck.

"*Do* stars really sparkle more at Christmas, Mother?" she persists.

"Yes," you tell her, "I think they do."

"I bet I know why."

"Okay, why?"

"Because it's a time when everybody *feels* sparkly when they look!"

"What's an Angel, Really?"

Angelic dialogue:

Seven-year-old, looking up from a Christmas card reproduction of Mabuse's famous painting *The Adoration of the Kings:* "What's an angel, really?"

"Well—a heavenly being."

"Angels can fly, that's sure. Wow, lookit those wings!" Studying the picture again: "They look like grown-up fairies. Bigger, though—they've got more clothes on, and bigger wings." Pondering: "When I die and go to heaven will I be an angel too?"

"Well, we think so, maybe."

"You mean I might *not* go to heaven?"

You laugh, and reply, though it sometimes seems doubtful: "Oh, no, I'm pretty sure you'll get there. Just that—we're not exactly sure what angels are. Anyway, your spirit will live on."

"I don't want to be a spirit, I want to be an angel, and get some wings so I can fly . . . wheee!" Then, "But angels have to sing good, don't they?"

"Maybe. Some of them. At least there was a heavenly choir singing to the shepherds the night Jesus was born."

"That's what I mean. Boy, I'd sure like to be in that choir sometime." The eyes are shining but the brow is troubled. "I don't sing very good yet. But d'you suppose if I try real hard and keep practicing, I might?"

"Yes, honey, of course, but what's the hurry? It will be a long time before you get to heaven and maybe audition for an angel choir."

"Well, I'm going to try out if they have one, that's sure. And if I do live a long time, that'll give me a lot more practice, so by then I should sing *real* good. Good enough to sing for Christmas!"

"I'm sure you'd be perfect, honey. Welcome in any choir . . . But I wonder if angels do sing anymore to announce the birth of Jesus? They don't have to—at least not to shepherds on hillsides, not where people can hear them."

"Okay, but they still *sing,* don't they?" he protests. "I'll bet they're just so happy around Jesus' birthday, they all get together and sing!" He gazes at the card, eyes shining. "And maybe that's why we're happy too. We can sort of feel them singing up there, and even hear them too, sometimes . . . *I* can—can't *you?*"

You nod and smile and touch the cowlicky head. "I certainly can." In fact, a small blond wingless angel has put a new but very old song in your heart right now:

Joy to the World!

Whimsical Sights and Sounds

Whimsical sights of the season . . .

A man in a red stocking cap on a motor scooter, merrily whizzing home with his Christmas tree . . .

A package-laden little girl pausing at a large street donation kettle. Carefully setting down her bundles, she opens her purse, digs out a little tin bank, and holding her gloves in her mouth, pries it open. The coins she has saved make a merry jingle as they are dumped into the kettle so that less fortunate children can go shopping too. . . .

Sign on a tree lot: SANTA'S CHRISTMAS FOREST. . . . And a young father and mother and three small fry trudging along the needled lanes, each youngster carrying a gaily nodding rubber reindeer . . .

A husband on a roof adjusting the lights around a manger scene while his pretty wife in a bulky sweater, calls suggestions from the sidewalk . . .

Christmas tree salesmen gathered around glowing oil drums getting warm, like shepherds crouched before their fires on a starry hillside long ago.

The Small Fry Say

Two-year-old, toddling to the window and gazing out astounded at a world newly covered with snow: "Who *did that?*"

Seven-year-old: "When I grow up, I'm

going to be one of those Santa's helpers and get to hold all those pretty girls on my lap!"

How You Can Tell It's Christmas

Things that sparkle at Christmas . . . Starry skies and children's eyes. Tinsel on trees, snowflakes in a breeze.

Things that crackle at Christmas . . . Ice underfoot. Fires on the grate. Paper on packages.

Things that jump at Christmas . . . Children at parades and in front of store windows. Jack-in-the-boxes. Fathers caught trying on Santa Claus costumes.

Things that squeal at Christmas . . . Little girls with excitement, new dolls being hugged.

Things that are warm at Christmas . . . Mittens from Grandma. Houses after sledding. Hugs and kisses. Hearts for each other.

The Mystery and Magic of Christmas

"Why is Christmas so special?" a child asks. "We have lots of other holidays, but people don't get excited like they do at Christmas. Christmas just seems more *wonderful!*"

This is true. In almost every country throughout the world, this holiday, whatever its actual date or customs, is celebrated with a fervor and joy known to no other.

Is it because birth is itself a miracle and a wonder? Any birth—a calf, a lamb, a kitten. And most mysterious and wonderful of all, the birth of a child.

To see any newborn baby, even through a hospital window, is to want to laugh and also, somehow, to cry—so tiny, helpless, pure and unsuspecting of life's complexities and problems. You want to cuddle and protect it. And yet just to witness its perfection is to feel oddly purified.

And the miracle of the Christ Child! . . . Christmas allows us to gaze in awe through the windows of the stable. To see the child of hope, of promise, the child who came to change the world.

It is as if through him the whole mystery of creation is revealed. Not explained away, but *revealed* for the eternal marvel that life is.

And this lovely mystery of Christmas is important: A virgin girl and her Annunciation. The gentle, protective Joseph. The angels, the amazing star. The Three Wise Men who followed that star so far.

There are those who would belittle and rob us of all this. Who deny the Virgin Birth, explain away the star. There are some modern scholars who do not regard the Magi as historical personalities, but rather as a genre of Jewish writing which dramatizes an idea through the creation of a story. But, thank heaven, the dry erudition of self-elected authorities and scholars hasn't riddled and ruined Christmas.

Its magic is too strong, its mystery too profound.

The mystery that floods our hearts with good will. That makes us, like the Wise Men, travel long difficult journeys, bearing gifts, just to be with those we love.

Let us keep the mystery and magic in Christmas. Surely it is this that makes Christmas so wonderful, so exciting, a holiday like no other.

Chapter 2

OF GIFTS
AND GREETINGS

In Praise of Christmas Letters

D eck the house with boughs of holly, 'tis the season to be jolly! I'm about to write our family Christmas letter: that glowing inventory of the year's events I've been saving up for the whole year. And as I pull the chair closer to my desk, it warms my heart to know that all over the country other people are as eagerly counting their blessings as they sit down to write theirs.

Never mind that Christmas letters have

gotten bad press lately. "Brag sheets" they've been called. "Boring reports that nobody reads." Well, let the scoffers scoff, the Scrooges sneer. To me the annual exchange of these letters is one of the happiest customs to appear on the American scene. Not everyone writes them, but for those who do, they are a song of hope and joy in this troubled world, proclaiming that despite the trials that beset us all, each year of life is to be treasured. God is good!

Christmas letters also serve two useful purposes. First, they can forge a vital link between friends who don't want to lose each other. Second, your own letters, if you save them, will provide a record of life for your family, each one a small but shining chapter in its biography.

I began to write ours years ago. My husband had been transferred often by his company. In each city, wherever they sent him, there were always two or three couples who became especially dear to us. As we moved and the numbers grew, correspondence became impossible; we came to rely on notes scribbled once a year on Christmas cards. Finally I ran out of time and space even for notes, giving up one year in frustration after getting only as far as the M's on our list. It was either drop everybody, except for impersonal greetings, or find a better way.

Christmas letters were just getting started. We had received a few and were delighted, devouring every word. What a great idea. It might be fun as well as feasible to write our own.

Nothing has been more rewarding. Most of our friends began to respond in kind, and along the way new ones joined the parade, bubbling over with their news, until now it's a happy avalanche. Some of them are too long to read all at once, but they're always welcome, always savored, even if later, a few at a time. No matter that I don't know half the people they speak of, and can't hope to keep their children and grandchildren straight. What *matters* is that they haven't forgotten us. They are reaching out to us across the miles and the years, sharing their joys and their sorrows, believing that we still care enough about them to want to know.

To me this is life-enriching. I feel sorry for people who miss it. And I grieve for the loss of once-close friends who let all this slip away.

Among the Scrooges who would take the

joy out of Christmas letters was a critic who wrote to Ann Landers, setting out rules for us eager innocents who write them. "Keep them short," he ordered. "Never more than a page. *Don't* describe your travels. And *never* send to people you don't know well."

Nuts! Cram the year's wonders onto a single page? You might as well tell Santa to travel light by dumping out half his toys. True, the shorter your letter the more likely it is to be read. But why spoil your own fun? And while you needn't make your Christmas letter a travelogue, we've done a lot of excellent armchair traveling with good friends. My husband and I save the longer, more colorful accounts to read aloud after the holidays. We've gone on African safaris with the Williamses, climbed the Alps with the Olsens, joined the Loschers on their visit to the Great Wall of China. We are thrilled for them and *with* them. There is vicarious pleasure in sharing their adventures, just as we feel they will take some small pleasure in sharing ours.

As for that edict about being very choosy about who gets your Christmas letters, nonsense! Let your heart prevail, along with your common sense. I have exchanged such letters with people from all walks of life, sometimes after a brief but somehow meaningful encounter, and occasionally with a reader or a writer I've never met.

Years after we moved away, the holidays were always brightened by a long newsy letter from the dear little Polish lady who used to sell us vegetables from her roadside stand. She loved us enough to know we'd always be interested—in the *kolacky* she was baking and boxing to send away to children now in college, the honors they were winning, the progress of her husband, war-crippled but always cheerful in his wheelchair. And as long as she lived, we responded in kind.

Every year I look forward to the letters of a Washington taxi driver who dropped me off at an autographing party one day and then dashed home to bring his wife. This man, Irving Schlaifer, has become a modest celebrity for his long Christmas letters detailing the small wonders of another year. Though he will give you a cab's-eye view of the state of the nation, and sometimes mention a notable just delivered to the White House, mainly it's the deal he got on a new car that's exciting—the sheen of its polish and the miles it gets to the gallon. It's celebrating another anniversary with Emma, the exact location of the beautiful restaurant where they dined, and the wonderful things on the menu. ("For dessert Emma chose cherries flambé. I decided on good old apple pie.") Frequently he includes the recipe for Emma's famous fruitcake, with this year's variations, and always, always, the names and antics of their family of cats.

Irving's letters are unique in their minutiae; few of us have time to write so much. But everybody on his long list adores them. Irving epitomizes the basic enthusiasm of the Christmas-letter writer, saying, in essence, "I'm proud of my job. I love my life and I love you. Here are my adventures. I hope you enjoy them. If not, I won't know the difference, but they've been fun for me!"

Adventures in living—that's what Christmas letters are all about. Most of them are joyful. I can't remember ever reading one that was filled with self-pity, doleful doings, or complaints. Not because we're being brave, or just reluctant to admit our failures, pain, and problems, but because at this season such things somehow dwindle in significance, lose their sting. Even the times when we must include important news such as divorce or a death in the family, these are related in terms of tenderness, faith, and hope for the bright new year.

No, at Christmas it isn't the burdens we long to express, it's the glow within us, the bounties and blessings. The achievements, the pleasures. And if some people are offended by reading of other people's happiness, in what they may consider "brag sheets," I'm not. I applaud. They are not meant to make me envious or affronted; they are paying me the compliment of believing that their news will be welcome. And as a friend I will rejoice.

But quite apart from other people's reactions to your Christmas letter, the truth is, you're not writing them for other people, *you are writing them for yourself.* You are harvesting these memories for the sheer joy of hugging them to your heart again, fixing them in time, setting them down. And if you keep them, they will be a rich harvest of memories for your family as well. Your Christmas letters can become their history. One-sided, yes, leaving out most of the troubles, but important in their statement that no matter what else may have happened during those difficult years, our life together was good.

I realized this recently when, in a box of old files, I found copies of some of our Christmas letters, many of them written long ago. Fascinated, I sat on the floor, reading all afternoon. . . .

The year I was rushed to the hospital the week before Christmas to deliver our baby girl (described in loving detail): "We brought her home on Christmas Eve. The kids had helped their dad trim an enormous tree in the window; its colored lights were shining on the snow. Everybody gathered around, eyes sparkling as we unwrapped the precious bundle (her eyes were sparkling too, we're sure). But I'm afraid the boys were just as excited over the TV set Santa had brought early (our first) as they were over their new baby sister. . . ."

Again: "Mark, thirteen, is busting his buttons. His picture made the Washington *Evening Star* with his 100-pound marlin, the biggest caught so far this year. . . ."

Paper routes and Scouting, dancing lessons, cheerleading, the year Mickie was prom queen, the graduations from high school or college. Moves, promotions, trips, remodeling a house, the thrill of a book or story sold.

On and on I read—events large or small, things I'd almost forgotten and which at the time probably meant little to anybody else. But oh, how important they were to us!

So many of those letters are missing. How I wish I had saved them all. But there are enough to gather together, every one I can find, and bind into booklets for my children. To refresh their memories, to read and laugh about and cherish, perhaps to pass along.

That first Christmas, while the heavenly chorus sang, the angel proclaimed the birth of Jesus, saying, "I bring you good tidings of great joy, which shall be to all people!" Our Christmas letters are our hearts' carols proclaiming, "Joy to the world! We've made it through another year and life is good!"

Surely this is a beautiful thing.

Apron-Pocket Philosophy

Every year practically everybody quails before the burden of a constantly snowballing Christmas card list. But actually we probably shouldn't complain. It only means that we're making new friends faster than the old ones are disappearing or dying off!

His Very Own Card

The years of the starry eyes . . .

"My card—where's my Christmas card?" the little one asks, rushing in from play.

"Your card? Let's see." You shuffle in vain through the mountainous stack. Where, among all this outpouring, are you likely to find one lone Christmas card? Feeling guilty, you choose one at random and offer it up. It *could* be his, you rationalize, and he won't know the difference anyway.

It isn't—and he does. "No, no, my card was blue with angels on it. Three angels," he insists. "One was singing, one was telling the shepherds the news, and one was baby-sitting."

"Baby-sitting?"

"Sort of, he was watching over baby Jesus. Only Mary was there—she had on a blue and white dress. And Joseph—" he ponders. "I forget what he was wearing. But there was a cow and a donkey and some little gold figures and it said—"

You gasp. "You even remember what it said?"

"I think so. Sister read it to me." Thoughtfully, " 'May the light of this little child shine upon you and bring you joy through all the year!' So you see, Grandma meant that just for me. I've just *got* to have my card."

"Indeed you have." Diligently now you search and produce it for him, watch him take it with reverent hands. His card, his very own card. Which he props before him as he lies on his stomach before the fire.

You regard the small, rapt figure lost in the wonder of his single card. Then you turn to the great basket of greetings, so full they are spilling over. Welcome cards, yes, but not really seen, or savored—many not even read. A sense of sadness touches you, plus a burst of delight. It is as if "the light of this little child" has flooded your being. Each card has suddenly become special, precious, a thing you can look forward to.

Let Your Gift Be a Symbol of Love

Gifts are as varied as the people who give and who receive them. And their value can only be measured by the joy that is known by each.

A first-grader's gift of a potholder made for Mommy, or lopsided clay elephant for Dad can hold more love and excitement than a diamond bracelet bestowed on a movie star.

A gift can be large, a gift can be small. A gift can be something dreamed of and saved for for months. Or it can be something unexpectedly spied in a store window, a thing so charming, so perfect an inspiration that you rush in to claim it, knowing it's the only gift that will do.

A gift can be something you want very much and sometimes even ask for. "You got it, you *got* it—oh, I know what it is!" The cry goes up as eager fingers rip the wrappings off. . . . Or a gift can be a total surprise. "For *me?* Oh, no, I just can't believe it!" Sometimes a gift is a remembrance from someone you scarcely know—a pitcher for your collection from that dear little lady you met at the antiques show: a loaf of nutbread from the woman whom you helped at the church bazaar.

A gift can be a service—the gift of your time, your hands. Baby-sitting for a busy mother so she can have one blessed day all her own. Giving a home permanent. Sewing. Cooking and serving a meal. Or a husband's refinishing one of his wife's old walnut tables, or building the bookshelves she's wanted so long.

A gift can be a luxury, something truly elegant you'd never dream of buying for yourself. Perfume or a swish negligee—or a rare item for a man's hobby, an expensive fishing rod.

Or a gift can be something practical—an

iron, a sweeper, a tool for Dad. Something that's used every day to make work lighter, and in the using be itself a reminder of the person who provided it for you.

A gift can be a treat: Dinner and the theater. A concert. A trip. . . . And a gift can be money, a check or a crisp new bill to be spent headily exactly as you please.

A gift has added meaning when it's that special something that only those who know your tastes would understand and take the trouble to find: That plant. That book, that record, that gourmet spice.

"The gift without the giver is bare," it has been said. And no matter what the gift—luxurious or practical, service or tool or money or treat or time—to be successful it must be wrapped in the shining substance of love. And the person who receives it will feel his heart beat a little faster, knowing that the gift is that love symbolized.

Who Says a Gift Has to Be New?

Most of us think all gifts must be spanking shiny new. We spend precious time and money in gift shops and crowded stores. We have the selection fancily wrapped and shipped off, insured as to actual material value, but with no insurance that the recipient doesn't already have half a dozen like it (or that he or she might not want even one!).

But did you ever think about giving someone dear to you something very old? Today, when even brides are beginning to be excited about antiques, why not select a piece of glass or china or silver from your own usually overstocked shelves?

Not long ago my mother, unable to get out and shop for a gift for a daughter-in-law, was fretting, when my sister suggested: "The carnival glass!"

"Oh, dear, but she knows I have it, she's seen it."

"Yes, and she's mad about it." And my sister Gwen got it down from the cupboard, and washed it up—the sparkling orange bowl, the six little sunset-bright punch cups. "Gee, think what you'd have to pay for this in an antiques shop!"

They nested it in tissue paper, wrapped the box gaily, and wrote this accompanying card: "If I could have gotten downtown I'd have bought you a nice new handkerchief or a box of stationery. Since I couldn't I'm giving you something old and used. I hope you're not disappointed."

"Disappointed?" screamed my sister-in-law when she lifted its loveliness to the light. "I'm so thrilled I could cry!"

So she was happy. Mother was happy. The people who admire it twinkling on the table are happy. And I think maybe the once cheap and gaudy treasure that was hidden away so long is happy too.

Of Children and Christmas Bazaars

Children are born bargain-hunters especially at Christmas. Just let a church or school bazaar come up and they are off to the white elephant table, a feverish love-light in their eyes and piggy-bank savings in hand. For where, oh, where could you find a gorgeous bracelet for Mother for fifty cents? Or a pen-knife for Dad for a dollar?

Grandma mustn't be forgotten, either; look at this lovely vase, only slightly cracked, for an incredible dime!

Like bees before a honeypot they hover, scooping up prizes, buzzing and exclaiming over them. "Look, Gracie, just look what I found—oh, don't let Judy see; it's for her, a purse, just like new, with a mirror in it even. I just can't *believe* it's only a quarter, can you?"

Shivering with excitement, they count out their coins, stuff their shopping bags, and lug them from table to table, pausing every now and then to dive into their depths and exhibit some incredible find to a friend. They are alert, however, lest mothers and fathers notice, keeping delicious guard over these discoveries that will later wind up under the Christmas tree. The bargains are so stupendous, they drift back again and again to see if there's something they missed.

At home little huddles with various members of the family take place. You hear the excited whisperings: "A little Scotch tape will fix it—" "I can cover that with a Magic Marker—" "I don't think the chip will show, do you? Now, don't you tell!" . . . And you feel a twist of something in your breast—a kind of exasperation along with a laughing clutch at the heart.

You think of all the shelves and drawers you rejoiced to clear, the bags and boxes of junk that were lugged to that selfsame center to become "fabulous bargains" in other innocent, shining eyes. And you brace yourself for this inevitable returning of the bread upon the waters. For it is, after all, the bread of love.

"Why, yes, it's perfectly beautiful!" you exclaim when you're consulted. "I'm sure Brother will be crazy about it. And you say it was only a quarter? What a wonderful shopper you are!"

Gifts Are for Loving—and Using

"Oh, they did fit, you can use them!" a relative exclaimed, seeing the India prints she had sent us adorning couches at the cabin. And her delight actually surpassed ours.

Gifts are so tricky. Their buying can be a burden. ("Oh, dear, Christmas comes too often," we protest. And, "No, no, not *another* wedding present!") But most of us set forth, if not always eagerly, at least cheerfully to find them. Trudging from store to store to make what seems the perfect selection, frequently spending more than we can afford. And despite the thank-you notes which courtesy demands, it's nice, so very nice, to have some proof that our choice was welcome. And doubly sad when all this effort fails.

A bride laughingly confided that she and her groom had played catch with a "horrible vase that somebody sent us. It was just too awful, we hoped we'd break it!" I hurt, for I knew the giver. Someone quite old, who'd asked her son to drive her shopping for something "especially lovely," and wrapped it herself and made a laborious trip to the post office to get it off.

It was almost a fetish with my mother to show appreciation for gifts. "Let's be sure and use the yellow tea set," she would say when Aunt Florence was coming. "She'll be so pleased." I remember her wearing a certain bracelet so that her friend could see it winking on her wrist; valiantly going to church in a not-very-becoming hat chosen by an eager son who'd bought it with money from mowing yards.

It was surely her spirit that sustained me when I carried to the hospital a too-tight bed jacket. A daughter had crocheted it in secret by the light of a flashlight after she was supposed to be asleep. The stamp of the beginner was upon it—but also the stamp of love. And I struggled into it somehow during visiting hours.

I think of my mother when viewing the acquisitions of Christmas: The many things a mother receives—from luxuries, to the homely items from the dime store or the efforts of a first-grader. What would she do about this slip that doesn't quite fit? This incredible umbrella? These potholders, these wild beads? Why, she'd praise them, love them, fix them if she had to—but above all, she'd *use them!*

What Becomes of Dolls?

"What becomes of dolls?" asks the father of two daughters. "Christmas comes, and birthdays—it seems you're always buying them. And friends and relatives give them more. But I just got to wondering—what becomes of them all in the end? What becomes of dolls?"

What becomes of dolls? You ponder. Well, there's the "collection," of course, kept behind glass in a cabinet (except when enchanted little faces peer too wistfully in). Character dolls, getting mothy and a little down-at-heel after all these years. Foreign dolls, frayed from many trips to school bazaars. And those non-such souvenir dolls people are always concocting out of straw, pecans, or old golf balls.

There are those few survivors in the attic—Dorothy, a lumpy, faded figure made from a flour sack pattern by a doting grandma. One of the original Shirley Temples, though the famous curls are matted, and a couple of teeth are missing. Happy, the clown, bedtime companion of which boy was it?

But whatever became of Viva, long-legged beauty of the curious name, that your eldest so long adored? What became of all the Marys, Susies, Bettys, Raggedy Anns that were so fondly bathed, fed succulent cakes of modeling clay, bundled up so proudly for carriage rides? (Or sometimes left out all night in the rain.)

Gone, vanished, lost in the mists of living, almost as the little girls who loved them subtly change and vanish in the business of growing up. . . . What becomes of dolls? Often we just don't know.

But again sometimes we do! When we go through toy cupboards with the children, deciding which ones can be parted with, which might actually profit by a new home. When we bundle them into boxes for the Scouts, the firemen, the church, or other groups of volunteers who, by adding a leg, a wig, a touch of paint, a dress, can make them good as new for Santa to deliver to somebody else. Perhaps another little girl who otherwise might not have a doll.

What becomes of dolls? It warms our hearts to know they are being loved again, bringing Christmas joy into other children's hearts.

The Gift That Multiplied

Roy worked for the service department of a large company in the city where we once lived. Although he had no children he always seemed to be broke and in debt. One day shortly before Christmas he confided to my husband: "This Christmas is going to be slim. I can't even afford the only thing Betty wants—for me to take her to the Ice Capades."

The next day he was exhibiting a fine new wallet he had just received in the mail. Saying nothing, my husband Lynn slipped a couple of bills into it—a twenty and a ten. When Roy got home he was astonished. Knowing the wallet had been empty, he called and accused my husband of the gift.

"Okay, so I did it," Lynn confessed. "Now don't argue, just take Betty to the Ice Capades!"

Across the street from Roy and Betty, however, lived a family who had lost a little girl, struck down by a car the year before. After talking it over, Roy and his wife decided what they really wanted to do with that precious thirty dollars. "If you don't mind," he explained, "we're going to buy a wreath for her grave. They have other children to provide for, and not much money. And this would mean so much to them. Betty and I decided we'd honestly get much more pleasure out of doing it than spending the money on ourselves."

My husband was so touched that he secretly suggested taking up a small collection. Not much—times were hard. "But at least enough so Roy can take Betty to that show." The other workers agreed, adding that it would be fun to surprise them.

To the men's delight, they raised not only enough for Roy's tickets, but to buy three more. "You know how they both love kids. If they want to, they can take the other children in that family *along* to the Ice Capades!"

The couple was ecstatic. After the performance they stopped by our house with their little flock, almost in tears as they tried to thank their co-workers already gathered there. "You've given us the happiest Christmas of our *lives*—!"

So a gift that began with an empty wallet multiplied, like the loaves and fishes, and spilled over into a lot of hearts.

A Mother's Wish-Gifts for Christmas

Lord, as I sit wrapping presents in this bright clutter of paper and ribbons beneath the tree, I keep thinking of other, better things I wish I could give my family.

First, I'd love to put peace, world peace in a package. But since I can't, maybe I can try even harder to keep peace within this house—to manage less hectic meals and bedtimes, to prevent or calm down its arguments and conflicts. Please help me in this, Lord.

And this fishing rod I'm struggling to wrap for my husband without revealing its secret, what would I like its clumsy package to include? Freedom to go fishing more often, for one thing. But

mostly freedom from worry—worry about mort-
gages and car payments, about our health, the
children's future, our happiness. As I sit here pondering this impossible gift, you make me realize I
can help by giving him my consideration, by doing
everything in my power to spare him.

Our sons, Lord, what would I like to tuck
into their boxes along with the boots and shirts
and football gear? For one son, self-confidence, be-
lief in his own abilities, more ease with girls. For
the other, better grades so he'll get into the college
he wants to attend. How can I compensate for
these gifts that I can't bestow? By continuing to
believe in my sons and showing it, I guess.

For my daughters, as I wrap the sweaters
and tennis racquets, the books and records, the doll
clothes I stayed up late to finish for my little one,
I can think of so much more I'd hand them if I
could. I'd like to give them poise and graciousness,
kindness and compassion, courage for all occasions—for tests and dates and interviews, but especially the courage to be themselves whether it
makes them popular or not. Above all, I'd like to
say, "Open your eyes and your arms to this priceless present: the wonder of being a woman today
when so many careers are calling and you can
still be a wife and mother if you want."

This list of my longings for all of them is

*endless, Lord. I can't wrap up the things I really
want, but one thing I can give all of them—
though no box would ever be big enough to hold
it. Something that's mine alone to give, as often as
I want:* my love.

Shopping Spree, Small Boy

The nine-year-old had been saving his
money for weeks, and actually earned a little
by running errands and sweeping porches and
walking neighbors' dogs. And he'd made a little list on a page of rough tablet paper, pondering and laboring over names, and asking
help with the spelling. And when I asked,
"Writing your letter to Santa Claus?" his eyes
sparkled. "No, no, something else"—sticking
it madly behind him—"you can't see!"

Then, unable to keep the secret: "It's my
shopping list. I'm going to pick out everything
all by myself this year, you can't even be
along."

"Dear, are you sure you'll have enough
money? And you might get lost."

He argued that his father had promised
him some extra. And he'll confine his foray to

Ida's, the friendly family-style department store on Georgia Avenue, not far away.

At last the day arrived. With many admonitions, "Now, don't lose your gloves or your money, and be careful crossing the street," I watched him trudge proudly off, a small, elated figure in a plaid jacket and dungarees. . . .

He returned at length, still rosy with delight, but clutching only a single sack. "Well, first I have to look at everything, don't I? Say, they're sure nice in that store; they don't care how long you look at things, or even if you touch them! They let you take your time."

"But what about all the other people on your list?"

"Oh, I'm going back tomorrow. I promised the clerks!"

The day before Christmas was busy. The sleigh bells on the door jangled merrily as people dashed in and out. There were parties, phone calls, cookies to be boxed and delivered, pals to be played with. But promptly at the usual hour of departure he was off to keep what he considered his sacred final tryst.

Nor was he wrong. Returning a little later, there was a new look of radiance on his face. "Well, I'm finished. I got everybody taken care of. And guess what?" He exhibited a gaily wrapped package. "This is for me!"

"For you? Dear, don't tell me you bought something for yourself?"

"I didn't have to," he beamed. "It's from the clerks. They'd seen me around so much doing my shopping, they called me over before I left and"—marveling—"they said they'd decided to give *me* a present!"

A Gift to Make a Man Feel Like a King

Moments that make marriage worthwhile . . .

The holidays always bring to mind a story that has nothing to do with Christmas—except that special Christmasy feeling that comes from an unexpected gift.

Especially when it has been bought out of a slender pocketbook and a sudden compelling fullness of the heart.

It is told by a friend of ours who is now an enormously wealthy man.

Working on a shoestring, he introduced the first locker storage plants in the Midwest, and made a fortune. But his particular "gift of the Magi" came before that, when he had married his high school sweetheart during the Depression.

He was running a filling station in their little town, and adding to their slender income by playing the tuba in the town band.

"One of the neighboring towns was having a Popcorn Festival, and the band was hired to play all day and during the evening. We got six dollars apiece, in advance.

"I saved my money, I didn't even eat. And walking down the street when we had a little time off, I saw a beautiful silver-plated tea service in the jewelry store window—and thought how thrilled Mary would be to have a set like that. So I went in and priced it, thinking it would be way beyond our means.

"But it was only twenty-seven dollars— the exact amount I had in my pocket! So I bought it and had them wrap it up real nice. And when we got through playing about eleven o'clock, I took it home to Mary. And there was never such a night in our lives!

"That silver meant more to us than anything we've bought since. We still have it, by golly. We use it in the kitchen. And I never see it that I don't recall the look in her eyes when she unwrapped it. It was one of those moments in marriage when a man really feels like a king!"

Let It Be a Merry Christmas for Everyone in the World

"Let's go downtown," the little girl clamors the day before Christmas. "It'll be our last chance to talk to Santa Claus!"

"Dear, you've already talked to him ten times in ten different stores."

"I know, but I've just got to see him. I've thought of a few more things."

"That's what I'm afraid of."

"Go on, Mother," says your eldest. "I'll tend to things. Get 'em out of the house," she whispers, "how can I finish those sports vests for Dad and the boys with everybody underfoot?"

"How can I finish the thousand things I've got to do?" you plead. But the day is crisp and sparkling, the temptation keen. "Okay," you recklessly announce.

To our surprise, the crowds that so recently surged the streets or jammed the aisles have disappeared. Except for a few harried last-minute shoppers, there is a leisurely feeling in the air.

You can gaze into the wonderland of windows without having to worm the children through or hold them overhead. "It's like having the place to yourselves," your little boy beams. "And lookit the bargains!"

Markdowns are everywhere. Dolls nobody wanted gaze wistfully back at you. There are bins and boxes of finds—tea sets, paints, puzzles in battered boxes, otherwise good as new. You find yourself—foolishly, to be sure—with a shopping bag crammed.

"C'mon, c'mon, let's go see Santa Claus now!"

Even that old gentleman can be interviewed without a long wait in line. And he has time really to listen to an eager little girl with stars in her eyes.

"Ha—Santa," scoffs the boy to prove he's finally accepted one of life's first disillusionments with his mind. But his emotions cannot yet make the change. He is pale, actually trembling as he perches his lengthening legs on the broad red knee. "Well, I want a dump truck, and a baseball bat—"

Good will is like music in the air. You wish Merry Christmas to the clerks, and they wish Merry Christmas to you. On the streets the little bells ring. "Thank you, dear, God bless you," the Salvation Army lassie smiles as the children drop their offerings in.

You fall into conversation with a poor but gentle man, on the bus, going home. "My kids won't have much this Christmas," he says, "but they be happy with what we give them. They knows I does the best I can."

Perched on her knees beside you, your little girl whispers in your ear, roots in the shopping bag. "These didn't cost much, we got them on sale," you explain as the youngsters ask him please to take these few little items home. "Tell them Merry Christmas from us!"

"Oh, my goodness. Oh, my, now, ain't that nice?" He keeps smiling at you and shaking his head. "It makes me wish I had something to give you."

Suddenly, as he reaches his stop, he plunges into his pockets, brings forth a dime for each of them. His eyes are shining as he waves at you from the street.

Hand in hand with your children, you go into your warm, bright house smelling of the fir tree in the window, the snapping logs on the grate. And a prayer keeps singing itself over and over in your heart: "Oh, God, let it be a Merry Christmas for everyone in the world!"

The Priceless Gift

Give me true generosity at Christmas, Lord. A generosity that doesn't get confused with pride or extravagance.

May this family's cards, our tree, our parties, our decorations, be all in the spirit of loving celebration of a glorious event, rather than the desire to impress.

Let me give with the zeal of my own children who will labor half the night to make something for somebody they love. Or who will spend every long-saved or hard-earned penny, not to show off, but because it is a glorious thing to give ungrudgingly, even at personal sacrifice.

Help me, above all, to remember that the family we honor and worship at Christmas were poor. Very poor. They couldn't have afforded a fine hotel had there been room. They were happy to take shelter in a hillside cave. They did not demand the best crib, the finest toys and garments for the child you sent. They were grateful to wrap him in swaddling clothes and place him in a manger.

God, fill me, too, with that same shining sense of gratefulness. So that it is not the price-tag-ridden emotions that dominate at Christmas, but joy in your priceless gift.

Grant me true generosity at Christmas, Lord. A generosity of spirit that is rooted in thankfulness.

Chapter 3

WITH THE CHILDREN

"Read Me a Christmas Story"

I t's time now, Mommy, Daddy. C'mon, get the books. Here, I've found some of them already—it's time to start reading Christmas stories!"

"My goodness, no, it can't be." (Impossible, adults always think. Why, it was only a few weeks ago that you were putting the last vestiges of Christmas *away*.)

But calendars don't lie. Nor the ardent vigil children keep toward holidays, nor the

excited conviction in their eyes. And they remember, all too well, the times you've put
them off with "Oh, my goodness, it's silly to
read about Santa Claus in summer. Wait till
it's cooler, till Christmas is really coming—"

But now a fire is snapping on the grate,
the wind is tapping at the door. You, too, are
suddenly aware of the hurrying feet of Christmas heading your way. It's time, it's truly time
to get acquainted with the jolly saint and his
elves, with all the pets and people who go
Yuletide adventuring once more.

"All right, everybody ready for bed?
Crawl in, here we go!"

Old favorites like *Birds' Christmas Carol*,
the Christmas chapters from *Five Little Peppers*,
Edna Dean Baker's beautiful *A Child Is Born*.
Early as it seems, the weeks will be all too few
to read them all before the climactic day—let
alone newer offerings from books and magazines. Such a feast of literary plenty, such a
tempting array from which to pick and choose!

And everybody must have *his* or *her* choice
and turn and the bedtime hour goes fast and
time is running out, and there are sometimes
quarrels.

And even older children who like to fancy
they've outgrown all this often stand in the

door, or stroll in to sit on a bed to listen. For nothing gives Christmas a more valid and glorious launching, or keeps its anticipation alive in the house, like this custom of bedtime reading. Especially when the best of all, the simple yet thrilling account of the Christ Child's birth as told in the Bible, is saved for Christmas Eve.

Give a Doll a Heart

"Let's make something for Christmas, something we can all make together, shall we?"

"Cookies?" you ask. "Tree trimmings, decorations for the house?"

"Well, yes, all that, too, but something special—well, say like dolls!"

"Dolls?" you groan. They've got to think of something—you're used to that. But does it always have to be so complicated?

"Sure, rag dolls. My goodness, Mother, we even made them in kindergarten!"

"I guess rag dolls wouldn't be too hard. Raggedy Ann and Andy!" you exclaim, inspired by some you've seen at a church bazaar. (Poor Johnny Gruelle; but then, he probably realizes it's only because his creations are so cunning that they're so widely plagiarized.)

You dig the two soiled but beaming figures from cluttered corners and trace a pattern off. Soon the sewing machine is happily suturing heads and legs and arms. *Why, this is a breeze,* you think as the flat figures multiply. And you lavishly visualize all the neighbors and the needy who will rejoice at your handiwork.

The children are already at the stuffing, though they've moved the operation to in front of the TV set. Needles, thread and gobs of cotton are all over the living room. Some of the heads are pretty lumpy, the limbs are too fat or too thin, and obviously this process will take longer than you reckoned. Nonetheless, you begin assembling assorted parts, and by midnight (long after they're in bed) two whole, if blank and hairless, dolls have been achieved.

"Now let's put their hair and faces on," the children urge the next day. "That's where the fun comes in."

It does. Although another whole evening is given over to looping on the bright yarn locks, the drawing and embroidering of faces, it's worth it when at last the jolly pair are twinkling at you with their black jet (just *try* to find authentic shoe buttons!) eyes.

They're still not dressed, however. And though the blue overalls and pinafored frocks look easy, they also take time. Meanwhile, however, the stuffing and the stitching continues. In fact, nobody dares to watch a program without some part of an Ann or Andy in his hands.

It becomes a kind of moral obligation now. Between cards and cookies and shopping and everything else, you are impelled to snatch up those grinning imps and inch them a bit closer to completion. And somehow, a week before Christmas, nine merry if somewhat bumpy Anns and Andys, fully clothed and finished (even to their painted hearts) are awaiting their destination.

Their destination? Someone to love them. And the youngsters say it for you: "Let's take them to one of those places—you know, where the dolls don't have to be so fancy but, if they don't get a lot, well—somebody might not get one!"

"That's it. Get on your wraps, that's exactly where they belong!"

The Christmas Baby

People feel sorry for Christmas babies, or those born near the holiday.

And rightly so; for it's just not possible to bring the same enthusiasm to a birthday that coincides with all the confusion and preoccupation of celebrating that other tremendous day.

Mark Twain, it is said, felt such sympathy for one such youngster that he grandly "gave" her his own birthday, which occurred much later in the year.

Yet despite the ensuing birthday party problems, the parents of a Christmas baby are uniquely privileged. We undergo an experience so memorable and beautiful that surely nothing else can ever surpass it: To hold a new baby in your arms at this holy season, just as Mary did. To feel the thrill of its tiny clutching fingers, hear the miracle of its cry—truly this is to see the brilliant star piercing the very heart of the stable, and to hear the angels sing.

And then to bring the new baby home in a scurry of blankets and gifts and good wishes, with holly wreaths on doorways and carolers in the street. Home to a warm, bright house where a Christmas tree is shining its welcome from a window, and friends and neighbors and other children gather about, enthralled. The special joy of new life joining a family, combined with the ecstasy of Christmas creates one of those rare occasions of perfection and significance.

It is one of the most beautiful experiences in the world.

"That's Our Tree!"

"When are we getting our tree?" the small fry begin to tease long before you're ready. "The Webers got theirs last night and are trimming it today."

"That's right, I've seen a lot of trees going past on my paper route. If we don't hurry, they'll be all gone."

"The earlier you get a tree up, the quicker it sheds," you argue. "We'll want it to last until after New Year's."

"That's right, I feel sorry for trees that people put up too early and then get rid of so quickly," the middle one protests. "They don't get to watch kids playing with their toys all through vacation, or get to enjoy New Year's Eve."

"That's silly," a brother hoots. "Trees aren't people, they don't care."

They seem like people though, when at last you do pile into the car and begin the search for yours. It can't be just any tree. It must be the fragrant balsam you always have. Any other would seem a stranger. And it must be ceiling-tall and full enough to sweep the floor. And its arms must be broad enough to hold the family accumulation of tinsel and lights and ornaments and home-made decorations.

The trees stand on the lots, row upon row, their branches rustling in the chill night breeze. "Take me, take me," they seem to say. But past them you go, trudging toward a likely candidate. Not tall enough or full enough, poor thing. "Thanks, anyway," you tell the friendly men crouched around the oil drums, where burning wood gives off a bright flame and an acrid, tangy smell.

And so back to the car that seems cozy after the cold foray. On to another lot, and another, until you begin to wonder if you are overchoosy. Or if, as one of the children voices it, appalled, "Wouldn't it be awful if we looked and looked and it got to be Christmas and we *never* found our tree?"

"Oh, we'll find it, don't worry."

Your husband pulls into a final lot, and there it is, bowing confidently to you at the very gates. *Your* tree. Your own perfect tree. The children recognize it at once and begin to dance around it excitedly, exclaiming, "That's our tree!" Your husband winces at the price but reaches gamely for his wallet. The attendant, a rollicking college boy bundled against the cold, helps to rope it to the car. You ride home with it crowning the top and trailing behind.

You pass other families whose trees jut from luggage compartments or wave gaily from the tops of cars. Tall trees or large, balsam or fir or pine, you know that they, as you, went on a very special quest tonight. And sought until they came upon it—their strange but familiar friend, like no other, waiting to join their circle, to reign in splendor and joy over their holidays. Their Christmas tree.

"Merry Christmas, Mrs. Scratch!"

~~ ~~ ~~

"A gingerbread house! Oh, please let's make a gingerbread house!" the second-grader pleads, racing up with a colored picture torn from papers unknown. At your expression: "*Sally's* mother always makes them a ginger-bread house every year."

You think frantically of the thousands of more vital things to do—cards, shopping, your own house in a horrendous state. But before this status symbol, you quail. "Well, let's see— if we've got enough gingerbread mix."

"Mix? *Sally's* mother makes everything from scratch."

"Sorry, but we're fresh out of scratch," you snap, marching toward the cupboard. "It's mix or else—"

"Then you will, you will!" She hurls her-self on you, rejoicing.

Naturally, there's no gingerbread mix on the shelf. Nor yet the molasses necessary if, like worthier, precivilization mothers you are prepared to go clear back to scratch. This means dispatching an older one to the store. Meanwhile, word has spread and eager little helpers have appeared: "I'm going to roll out the dough!" "No, me, me!" "I'm going to make the witch!" "I'll make Hansel and Gretel!"

"Witch? Hansel and Gretel?" You quail some more.

"Sure, like in the picture—see? Like in the fairy tale!"

You gulp, realizing too late that you have bitten off more gingerbread than you were prepared to chew.

And when the materials have arrived, and the dough is being thoroughly manhandled, spilled and fought-over, you consult the paper to discover: "Pattern and directions for making the house may be obtained by writing to—!"

But there's no escape now. Like Hansel and Gretel—or the poor witch they played that mean trick on, you, too, are oven-trapped!

Bravely you sketch a reasonable facsimile of the pictured house, and get out your cookie cutters. Prayerfully, you turn on the oven. Soon the spicy fragrance of baking gingerbread fills the air. Meanwhile, smeary children mix icing, color it, and prepare to spread it on everything they don't eat first.

It takes all afternoon, but eventually, perhaps through sheer Christmas magic, a shaky but intact gingerbread house is raised. A house complete with little figures and even a couple of surviving trees.

"Well, good-bye, thanks for helping," you say, shooing children home or to their baths.

Wearily you postpone the mess in the kitchen. You turn on a carol, plug in the lights that frame the doorway. And as you do a strange thing happens. The gingerbread house is light-flooded. And the old witch grins— you'd swear it. You can almost hear her muttering: "Merry Christmas, Mrs. Scratch!"

Angelic Rebellion—or, What Do Angels Wear?

"Mother, Mother, guess what? I'm in the program, they choosed me to be in the Christmas program at school!"

"Oh, fine, wonderful, what're you going to be?" Something simple, you hope. A wise man. That's easy—bathrobe, towel for turban, or maybe a head scarf.

He looks doubtfully at his brother. "An angel," he announces defensively.

"An angel! A *boy* angel! Oh, brrrrother, that teacher of yours must be nuts."

"I'm sure I don't know why," you declare.

"I'm sure there are boy angels just as well as girls."

"Sure, when little boys die they go to heaven, too, don't they, Mom?" the smaller one beseeches.

"I know one that won't," his brother grins.

"Now, now, now; who's talking about dying?"

"Yeah, but boys for *live* angels?" The older makes expressions of horror while the face of the younger one crumples. "Right up there on the *stage?*"

"That's enough," you decree, and scold the heckler from the room. "You'll make a fine angel. Now, how about costumes?"

Something white and soft and full, of course. You have it! Up in the bureau drawer. It would be perfect tied with a golden cord. You can see it already—so sweet, especially with halo and wings.

Your son is glowering at you now, his suspicions deepening. "Teacher hasn't said yet. But I know one thing—I *won't* wear anybody's old nightgown!"

"But, darling, why not? I mean—" Hopefully, "Sister has such a lovely one—"

He is weeping now; he stamps his foot.

"I won't; I won't be a darned old angel! They can't make me; nobody, not even if I was choosed!"

"Who else was chosen, honey? Weren't there some other boys?"

"Jimmy and Mikey and Butch," he sniffles, naming the three least angelic candidates in the class.

"Dear, if it'll make you feel any better, I'll call their mothers." Before you can reach the phone, however, it is summoning you. "Hello, this is Butchy's mother. What's this about their being angels? He's having a fit—"

By evening the angelic rebellion calls for an intercessor. Calling the teacher, you don't know whether to be let down or relieved.

"Oh, my goodness," she laughs, "they're just part of the angel chorus. They don't have to wear anything special. They just stand behind a cloud and sing!"

Party Invitations

It's fun to be a woman when . . .

Party invitations fly into (and around) the house like a flock of seasonal birds. They perch on windowsills, dive into drawers, even wander into cluttered closets. Some of them slyly nest among the bright jungle of Christmas cards.

They are exasperating little creatures, for all their bright colors and songs. You never can catch one when you really want him. "What time are we supposed to be at the Clarkes?"

"Three—I think. Or maybe it's five—if it's five I'll have to wear something totally different because after that we're due at Amanda's. At least I *think* her party is tonight—or is it tomorrow?"

"Better make sure. Tomorrow's out—the church pageant is tomorrow. Check the calendar."

"Oh, dear, I'm afraid I didn't write everything down."

"Okay, then, let's find the invitations."

It is at this point that the birds decide to disappear: The envelope that you *know* you propped on the mantel—even the one you pinned firmly to the window curtain—all, all have gone winging away.

All this complicated by the fact that the children are also clamoring, "I've got to go to Jimmy's birthday party—I forgot to tell you it's not just a Christmas party it's his birthday too. I've got to take him a present, what shall I give him, and who can take me?"

"Maybe Brother—he's going to something himself in half an hour. Where does Jimmy Lane live? And what time is his party?"

"I forget, it tells on the invitation—"

"Well, *find* the invitation!"

It's hectic, all this, but it's happy too. It's nice to have a time of year when suddenly everybody flings his door wide to friends and says, "Come, let's get together, let's celebrate!"

The Kittens That Couldn't Wait

Your pets and ours . . .

"Mommy, Mommy, come look!" our little girl exclaimed three days after Cinder produced a Christmas season quintette. "The kittens have their eyes open!"

"Oh, honey, no, they can't have, not yet. All kittens are blind for the first week or ten days. You know that."

"Well, maybe other kittens, but not these. C'mon, I'll show you."

She led me into the closet that was doubling as a maternity ward and squatted to take up a tiny bundle. Sure enough, it gazed at me, blank but wide-eyed.

"For goodness' sake!" I exclaimed, reaching for one of its brothers. "This one's eyes are open too—just barely, but certainly not shut."

I examined each twiggy, mewing newcomer. To my amazement, all except one were actually regarding their surroundings. Puzzled, I called the vet, who told me, "Are you sure you're not mistaken? I've never heard of such a thing."

"No," I told him, "their eyes are definitely open, and the blessed event occurred only day before yesterday." (With all the commotion that accompanies such an arrival, how could I forget?)

"Well, I can't explain it," he said. "Just take care that they don't get too much light and they should be all right."

I hung up, feeling strangely merry. "He doesn't know why," I told our daughter. "But we seem to have some precocious cats."

"Oh, I can tell you *why*," she informed me, cuddling one kitten close. "Just think if you were a kitty and it was almost Christmas. Wouldn't *you* hurry up and open your eyes so you'd be sure and see Santa Claus?"

Take Time for Christmas Memories

It is the day before Christmas.

The cookies are crisp in the kitchen and the last late cards have been mailed. The sleigh bells on the front door make clamorous music each time the children dash in and out. Then suddenly they are gone, the lot of them, husband and all, on those mysterious last-minute errands they always remember in the late afternoon. Except for a radio carol and the contented crackling of the fire before which our big dog dreams, I am alone in a house gone still.

Each of us has a moment when, if at all, the Christmas spirit seems to come rushing in, so poignant, so all-consuming, it is almost not to be held. For me, then, this is the time. The hour each year when I simply have to sit down and give the emotion full sway.

The symbols of Christmas are all about— the mistletoe, the holly. The tree graces the window like a shining silver queen. And sniffing its tangy scent (nature's own frankincense and myrrh), I ponder its significance. Just what do such symbols mean? Not in relation to ancient gods and customs—Hertha who danced in the smoke of burning boughs upon the hearth, the mistletoe that slew Balder the Beautiful and thereafter grieved for love—but to me and my household; in fact to all households.

And it comes to me that we find Christmas worthy of so much effort because it began first of all with a *family*. Man, woman, and child in a stable. A place that, however alien and humble, was for a little while their home. That perhaps is why this particular holiday has such power over parents' hearts. Why we yearn to shelter our young in houses made gay with greens and festive with lights. Why we gather them with us about snug fires, let them stuff themselves with sweets we normally would ration, and give them every gift labor and love can devise. Why, above all, we strive, whether consciously or not, to endow them with memories of home and Christmas they will treasure all their lives.

There are, it seems to me, two key ideas when it comes to creating enduring Christmas memories. The one: *Take time to enjoy it*. The other: *Let the family share in every phase*.

Why, for instance, does this particular tree at this moment fill me with such delight? Because it brings the family surging back into the house—my husband with his hat brim cock-eyed as he hauled it triumphantly through the door, our five-year-old impishly straddling a branch and trying to ride while his big brother attempted with equal vigor to drag him off. It brings back sounds of hammering and sawing in the basement as the three of them built its support. And the scene of its trimming, with teenagers munching popcorn from the strings and pitching icicles at daughter Mickie, perched precariously atop the stepladder, her hair as bright upon her shoulders as that of the angel she was clipping to a twig.

The ornaments on its branches recall our excitement when we came upon an old secondhand store and found them in a musty bin. Ancient discards from the days when churches had old-fashioned Christmas trees ceiling-tall. Fragile glass birds with tinsel tails, elfin bells, parasols, flowers, stars, a tiny carousel—a bit tarnished, true, a bit battle-scarred, but still a veritable treasure, the like of which is no longer seen. And we got the lot for a few dollars!

No, it's not this tree itself that any of us will remember. It will be all the trips to all the spicily scented markets to find, each year, the perfect one. It will be all the confusion and comedy of the trimmings. It will be the time the lights kept blowing the fuses, and the time the cat nearly pulled it over; it will be all the trees we've ever had and enjoyed because we've enjoyed them *together,* every phase of every one.

We know a very efficient family where the tree is ordered by telephone. "They send us choice ones, really," is the explanation, "and it saves all that bother of trailing around and picking out, to say nothing of getting them home." From a safe distance the children are allowed to watch the fireproofing and the spraying that will keep it from shedding—then shooed out while Mother trims. All day long she labors, carefully hanging each strip of silver, symmetrically attaching each bright ball. Finally, exhausted but proud, she summons the youngsters back to admire what is truly her work of art.

No lopsided arrangements here, no branches looking like overfeathered chickens, or skinny, half-plucked ones. No paper chains stickily pasted in kindergarten; no homemade bangles and doodads. But also, one can't help thinking—no fun!

This same woman is the joy of post office and clerks. She does her Christmas shopping early—during the August sales, in fact. Long before Thanksgiving all out-of-town packages are well on their way. Once I thought to emulate her example. But somehow it's hard to get the Christmas spirit when you can fry an egg on the sidewalk instead of frosting your toes. You find yourself thinking in terms not of what your loved ones might really want, but what's marked down. And later, when the papers begin to shout only so many shopping days left and the crowds begin to bustle—well, however smug you feel, there is also a sense of loneliness. Like getting to the party and home again before the guests arrive!

Then, too, a tie bought today and mailed tomorrow carries with it your own enthusiasm, your own fresh sense of value. But one that's been lying around three months! Is it as pretty, you wonder, as you first thought? Mightn't something else be better? Have you really got enough? And like as not, you'll find sufficient excuses to go barging right back and do it all over. At least I did.

Because I disagree mightily with those to whom Christmas shopping is an annual evil.

Let them streamline it all they will; let them settle for gifts of money or coupons to be redeemed. To me it's one of the most exciting and enjoyable adventures of the year.

Shopping as early as conveniently possible, so that you don't have to rush, will, of course, increase the enjoyment. Shop early in the day, if you can, while both clerks and stocks are fresh and aisles uncrowded. Learn to conserve your strength by having everything possible delivered. Simplify matters by having many of the out-of-town gifts wrapped and mailed from the store. We owe it to ourselves to take advantage of any services which minimize the minus side of shopping (the aching back, the irritations), and emphasize the plus: The sheer enchantment of store windows, the countless Santa Clauses lending patient old ears to the secrets of breathless, bright-eyed children all day long. Bing Crosby crooning a carol from a passing truck. The snow, the sparkle, yes, even the crowds.

A good deal of it must, of course, be done alone. You can't make much progress or truly enjoy it if you have to trail the youngsters along. But there are ways to dispose of them, and ways to include them as well. In small communities, merchants frequently stage free matinees for kids, leaving their parents unhampered shopping hours. In larger cities, many department stores provide well-staffed, delightfully equipped nurseries where the young fry can be parked without charge. Grandmothers are usually accommodating, when available. Or it's worth the price of a baby-sitter, if you can get one, to have even a single day on your own.

The children themselves, however, deserve their day downtown. Give it to them—and don't try to combine it with errands of your own. Keep the note of "Hurry, hurry, come on now" completely out. Let them gaze their fill at store windows with their animated reindeer and fairy tales and Mother Goose. Let them ride the little trains and go down the North Pole slide. Let them interview Santa Claus. Lead them up and down the aisles in search of presents for their friends; lift them up to counters, and insofar as possible let them choose.

Certainly it's a lot easier to avoid all this. Easier by far to summon, "See here, dear, this is what you're giving to Daddy; isn't it nice? And this is what I bought for you to give Mrs. Smith at Sunday School." But if you're serious about your children's Christmas memories, don't deny them this phase of it. Unless they're already tired and sniffly, the thrilling world of Christmas shoppers is likely to do them no harm. And the act of fishing a dollar from his own little purse and proudly handing it over gives a gift more significance to your boy or girl than a more expensive one that someone else provides.

When he is older, encourage him to earn his own Christmas money, and let him go it alone, if he likes. This past Christmas was a gala one indeed for our ten-year-old. Filthy rich from his first paper route, he sallied forth, stars in his eyes. Surely, he made mistakes. An extravagantly packaged lipstick for Sister—in the wrong shade (it was quietly exchanged). Another wallet for his dad, who has enough of them lying around now to start a store. But he also showed remarkable judgment in other instances. And his rosy excitement as he trudged home, package-laden, the glee with which he beckoned me to his room and locked the door before beginning his proud display told me as nothing else could that this was one Christmas he'd remember a long, long time.

There is an extra measure of enjoyment in the shopping you do with your mate. At our house, I generally buy the "sensibles." The pajamas and mittens and stockings and such which add to the total under the tree while replenishing everyday needs. But when it comes to the toys—well, it seems to us that's a matter for mothers and dads as a team. And we formed the habit of meeting somewhere for lunch or dinner first, making it a date. Letters to Santa studied together in a cozy restaurant have qualities of intrigue and delight that somehow go with Christmas, and go with love. There is something about these earnestly scrawled requests of the little people your union has created—especially when you are just a little away from them—that draws you close.

And while I could just as well buy the dolls and tea sets by myself (and save money—Lynn, my husband, always wants to spend more than I think we should), while he could decide about sidewalk bikes and football helmets just as well without a woman along—we *enjoy* these trips through *Toy Land* together. Goodness knows you worry about your offspring together; why not be happy about them together when this shining opportunity comes? For at no season is it more rewarding to be a parent than this when the electric trains are whisking round the tracks, and horns toot, tiny pianos tinkle, and dolls hold out their arms.

The family that joins forces to make much of its own Christmas equipment is investing in future memories: Of evenings spent around the dining room table, spatter-painting Christmas cards. Of hours stringing popcorn for the tree, or concocting ornaments out of jar lids and costume jewelry and foil-covered light bulbs. Of Saturdays in the kitchen, cracking nuts, baking cookies, making candy, stuffing dates. Of Sundays in the basement carpentering with Dad—a footstool for Grandma, a Cub Scout tray for Mom; or in the sewing room with Mother working on potholders or aprons or blouses.

Nearly every year we also make our own cards. For those we always like best to receive, the ones that go in the box "To Keep," are always those with a personal touch. Once, we cut up the want-ad sections of newspapers in the shape of Christmas trees. Then with red and green crayons we circled words and phrases that together formed a greeting. They were fun to fashion and, our friends said, fun to get.

Pictures of your home and family are always good. Many photo services offer these reproduced on a greeting card. We've found it even more effective as well as economical to order prints of a favorite snapshot, staple it into a construction-paper folder, and write our own sentiments in prose or rhyme.

One special Christmas, we combined baby announcements with holiday greetings, to wit: A snap of the three children extant waving from the porch of the huge old Victorian house we had recently bought and remodeled. Beneath them a lyric, which, if not exactly immortal, imparted both message and news. Space was left for name, date, and weight of the forthcoming new occupant of the old-fashioned house shown.

It proved to be a race between Santa and the stork, but fortunately the stork won. Our daughter dashed in the essential data, Mark stuck the folders into already addressed envelopes, Mallory licked stamps, and Lynn hurried them into the mails.

The possibilities for homemade cards are endless. They take only a little ingenuity, a few inexpensive materials, and the desire to make Christmas memorable. Yet they yield incomparable rewards in knitting both friends and family a little tighter into your heart.

Like most families, we had always decorated our house inside. Wreaths in the windows, boughs on the mantel, mistletoe brazenly draping every chandelier. But it just never occurred to us to decorate for the benefit of passersby; not even on those nights when we all piled into the car and drove around to enjoy and admire the outdoor effects of others.

Then we bought this immense old Victorian house at the corner of a busy thoroughfare. Painting it alone wrought such a miracle that people for blocks around actually called to thank us! Realizing then its inescapable prominence, we were inspired. Come Christmas, we would stick a few stars in the old gal's hair. We would drape her pillars and porches and balcony with a necklace of colored lights. And while we were at it, why not parade a few figures in silhouette across the roof?

The Three Wise Men seemed the most feasible to start. Copying from a Christmas card, I drew them first on a small sheet of paper, then blew up the design on wrapping paper almost to life size. Plywood would be a good material to cut them from, we thought. But as we prowled the attic, we found something even better, an old linoleum rug. It took the markings of the heavy crayon used to transfer the pattern, and was soft enough to yield quickly to the knife my husband used to cut the figures out. What's more, the undersurface was already black; we didn't even have to paint to get the silhouette effect—merely turn it over. Pieces of lath nailed to the back acted as braces. We had the whole thing made and set up on the porch roof in simply no time at all, barely a couple of hours.

With amber lights behind them, and riding toward a huge bright star, they proved so effective that we were frequently identified as, "Oh, yes, you're the people in the house with the camels!"

A small central balcony lent itself so perfectly to a manger scene that we cut another silhouette of Mary, Joseph, and the angel in a group there. And the next year we scared up enough linoleum to make the shepherds.

Such things take time, of course. But we've found that people do pretty much what they want to do in this busy world. If you really care about Christmas, if you honestly want to enjoy it to the hilt—well, you'll make or take the time for preparations. What is even more important, you'll set aside time for those events of the season which mean so terribly much to the children. That concert the junior choir is giving, the parties and programs at church and school. And if it should ever come to a choice between the preparations and the programs, let the preparations wait.

The cleverest cards in the world, the most elegantly wrapped gifts, the handsomest tree, are as nothing compared to that wonderful, terrible moment when your little boy marches onto the platform and anxiously scans the audience to see if you're there.

Equally important to children is their learning to share with others in this season of good will. As early as you can possibly get to it, have them help you clean out their closets and toy cupboards. Together select the garments which are good but no longer in use, to make some other youngster warm and glad. Broken toys and others which have merely lost their luster can go into bushel baskets to be mended by firemen and other agencies, made bright and whole again for youngsters whom Santa might otherwise have to skip.

Now, too, is the time to let them help you plan for CARE packages, to confer about saving for special offerings at church, to explain the meaning of Salvation Army bells ringing on the streets. Emphasize these elements at the very beginning of the holiday period. It will give your youngsters both a sense of appreciation for what they have, and a sense of responsibility to all mankind. It will establish concepts of Christmas as a time to ask not merely "What will I get?" but something far more important: "What can I give?"

The cornerstone of Christmas should be, of course, the family church. In these days, too often Santa's sleigh supplants the Christ Child's cradle, and in the dazzle of artificial lights we lose sight of his star. Fortunately, the church of our faith "came with" this wonderful old house (right next door). So there was ample chance to scurry together to all its services and activities, no matter how busy we were. But even if the effort were greater, we would not skip any part of this important relationship, that of the family to its church at Christmastime. For there the very essence of the holiday is to be found. There the origin of it all—the meaning of every generous impulse, warm greeting, every desire to love and share. There, indeed, that miracle without which even the festivities and bedeckings would be pointless and false.

Another way to make Christmas remembered is to read together some of your favorite Christmas stories. We save that most simple and thrilling one of all, the account of the Christ Child in the Bible, for Christmas Eve itself. These bedtime sessions have a magical way of making Christmas seem the most wonderful thing that ever happened to the world— as indeed it is! *And what snug memories they will surely summon when our boys and girls are men and women, grown and gone to homes of their own.*

During the last week before Christmas, as the schedule of other affairs permits, we try to set aside certain evenings for certain things. Gift wrapping, decorating, or trimming the tree. We're not too strict about it; there are frequent interferences, overlaps of activity, and changes of mind.

We also devote one of these nights to a kind of open house for the kids. Not exactly a party; no formal invitations, no gift exchanges, and nobody comes dressed up. But word goes out at school and through the neighborhood that we're going to show movies, and they're welcome to come. A dramatized " 'Twas the Night Before Christmas," cartoons, and some of our own home movies of previous Christmases are the usual fare. Mark proudly operates the projector; Mallory struts around with cookies and pretzels; their dad or I or big sister Mickie serves punch. It's a painless form of entertainment (if you have strong ears and don't mind crumbs on the rug) and one the children always look forward to and love.

Customs, traditions, the special ways you always celebrate Christmas at your house. Such are the framework for memories that endure. And as such I think every young new family should establish traditions and customs of its own. I think it a pity when Christmas has to be spent one year with *his* folks, the next with *hers,* so that no cozy patterns for their own Christmas can ever quite take root.

The customs of Christmas at *our* house are not particularly colorful or unique. Scrambled eggs and sausages eaten before a blazing fire in the living room Christmas Eve. A stocking hung for Spooky, our dog, along with the rest. A little table set with crackers and milk for Santa Claus—and the note of thanks he always remembers to leave. Church services at midnight. Movie taking in the morning, while still in our pajamas. A Jack Horner pie in the late afternoon. Nothing very important or unusual, but precious to all of us.

Take time to enjoy it. Let the whole family share.

It was one very special Christmas that I realized, as never before, what both phrases could mean. Heavy with the coming baby, trying to fill those last eternal weeks of waiting, I had plenty of time to savor every phase. And when at last the hurried good-byes had been said, when I heard the little new voice crying and held the miracle in my arms, I felt very close to that first Christmas family long ago— and to my own. For I knew that when we got home this day-before-Christmas, baby and I, all the things I had left undone would be accomplished. The tree would be shining, the cards would be out, the camels would be journeying toward their lighted canvas star. My husband and the children would attend to everything. After all—hadn't they always helped?

Look About You and Behold

A baby is a thing of beauty
No matter what its race;
Innocence and childhood
Are twins that kiss its face.
Babies plant a special hope
Within the human breast;
And courage cradles every birth
While love provides its breath.
There was a baby long ago,
The Fairest of the Fair—
Look about you and behold
His Beauty everywhere!
    —Hope Good

Aftermath

The nurse in noiseless rubber soles
Comes treading silent as a nun,
A squirming bit of human life
Sheltered in white within her arms.
From corridor of hospital
The racing feet no longer matter;
Within the room a gentle calm
Surrounds the Miracle completed.
Within this calm the sweetest sound
Echoes again—the voice
Of God's own gift to woman.
                    —Cleo Jackson

A Baby in Swaddling Clothes

"And she brought forth her firstborn son and wrapped him in swaddling clothes, and laid him in a manger—" (Luke 2:7)

Swaddling clothes . . . Mothers preparing for the arrival of their babies—smoothing the birdseye, feather-stitching the soft flannel—often think of the term as a baby's first little garments—shirts and kimonos and diapers and the now-passé tummy bands.

True, we know from pictures that the infants of Jesus' time were wrapped, instead, in linens. "Swaddled," or bound.

But few of us have ever stopped really to wonder why babies were clothed in this manner. "Here I am a minister's daughter," a friend related not long ago. "But only recently did I become curious enough about this custom to inquire."

Her own minister, when consulted, was a trifle taken aback. He'd never troubled to inform himself either. Encyclopedias didn't even refer to it.

One Bible dictionary called it simply "a bandage or band."

Another described the procedure: "The infant was placed diagonally on a square piece of cloth, the ends of which were turned over the body and the feet and under the head and fastened by bands tied around the child thus wrapped."

A third vouchsafed the reason: "To prevent free movement. Now chiefly referring to the earliest period of life when action is restricted."

My friend also discovered, to her amusement that "swaddler" was a term applied to early Methodist ministers—"Because they restricted certain actions in their flocks?" she conjectures. And later to any Protestant minister.

"But I still had no clues as to why this was done," she continues, "until quite by accident I came across an article in some little publication about ancient customs and beliefs in regard to childbirth.

"And in it was cited the ancient Jewish practice of binding the newborn infant so that his feet would become straight and he would 'walk upright.'

"Shortly thereafter our first grandchild was born prematurely. And his little limbs were crooked. And his parents had to consult a specialist so that he, too, might 'walk upright.'

"To everyone's surprise, the doctor was so busy that they had to wait a month for the appointment! None of us had realized before how common the situation is, even in full-term babies.

"Usually nature takes care of this matter of straightening the feet. Sometimes—as in the case of a friend of ours—the child has to wear braces. Fortunately our baby is being helped by wearing corrective shoes.

"But the true significance of swaddling has finally come home to me. This very human problem must go back down through the ages even to Bible times.

"Even Mary, who bore the Christ Child, was aware of it, and being a good mother, wrapped her child, as was the custom, in swaddling clothes!"

I'm so glad to know this. And my friend and I agreed. Understanding that custom seems to make that cold, long-ago night just a little bit closer to us.

They Come in, Cold and Laughing

They come in, cold and laughing, the other couples who are going to the dance with your teenage daughter and her date. Their eyes are bright with anticipation, their cheeks are flushed, nonsense bubbles lightly from their lips.

The girls' hair falls soft about their shoulders, dances in nimble ponytails, or crisply feathers their faces. In it they've stuck tiny sprigs of mistletoe or holly.

As a concession to the occasion, they're wearing stockings, but their feet are encased in the flat shoes they all wear with such casual grace.

The boys seem younger than the girls, although they aren't. They are a little stiff and uncertain in their ties and jackets; they laugh with more restraint.

Your husband comes cheerfully up from the basement, where he is making copper gadgets for Christmas gifts. He is wearing an old blue shirt and a pair of disreputable trousers, but his face is almost as young in its radiance as that of the kids.

While he's upstairs getting the car keys, one of the girls briskly and inaccurately plays Christmas carols, and with blissful lack of harmony the others sing.

Meanwhile, your daughter flashes about doing last-minute things—finding a lipstick, fastening some tiny silver bells to the hem of her skirt. She's a trifle nervous and hurried, but smiling, and as you bend near to help fasten her pearls, she smells like a rose.

Little folks, realizing the car is leaving, beg to ride along, and "Sure, okay, let 'em, we'll hold 'em!" the older ones surprisingly say. There is a sudden avalanche out the door.

Even the toddler bobs excitedly up and down, exclaiming, "Bye-bye, car-car—tum on, hoowy up!" and plunges through the departing legs. Somebody scoops him up and he, too, disappears.

And now except for the TV going strong, the house is quiet. But still vibrating with the young personalities that have filled it to overflowing. Still warm and bright and lived-in, clutter and all.

And standing there in its center, you think—this is it. The best time of life for a woman. And you long to hug it to you, enjoy it to the hilt, at this, the very best time of the year!

Chapter 4

CHRISTMAS, A TIME FOR CARING

Our Love Has Many Faces

"Though I speak with the tongues of men and of angels, and have not love," says Paul's famous chapter in First Corinthians, "I am become as sounding brass, or a tinkling cymbal." And he goes on to list the many virtues and good deeds that are empty and meaningless unless the motive is also genuine love.

These we could paraphrase in the hectic days before Christmas: "Though I address a thousand greetings, buy and wrap the most expensive presents, give the finest parties, cook the biggest dinners . . . if I do any of these things for any reason except love, they profit me nothing."

Yet, to be quite honest, most of us are simply swept into the lovely chaos of Christmas, and find ourselves functioning from sheer habit. And though "love envieth not"—we do envy. "Love vaunteth not itself"—yet, let's face it, we do strive to impress.

To combat this, a charming gentleman, Paul Rankin of the British Embassy, proposes: SCROOGE (Society for the Complete Riddance of Obsolete and Onerous Greeting Exchanges), its members to be relieved of the expense and burden of Christmas cards; the money saved to be donated to some charity such as Children's Hospital or homes for needy children. "Think of all the Tiny Tims we could provide crutches for—or the families for whom we could buy a goose! It might even become a status symbol—to belong and *not* send Christmas greetings."

Mother Always Said

❧❧ ❧❧ ❧❧

"You can't 'keep Christmas'—you've got to give it!"

The Gift of Caring

❧❧ ❧❧ ❧❧

Dear Lord, don't let me be so busy with my own selfish projects at Christmas that I neglect people less lucky than we are.

There is so much suffering everywhere. So much loneliness. It weighs on me even as it enhances my own sense of being richly blessed. I hear the Salvation Army bells tinkling on the street.

"Remember the friendless, remember the poor." And hurry guiltily past. Or I drop something in the kettle and feel better—suddenly filled with love. But you know and I know that such gestures aren't enough.

Yet where to start? How can any of us make even a dent in this vast need? A part of me protests. Resists. "No, no, I can't. With so many demands already, how can I do any more?"

Then you remind me that you know each of

our limitations. You never expect more than we are ready or able to give. You make me aware that we needn't go too far from home to begin.

That housebound old lady in the next block. I will call on her myself.

The nearby settlement house, the hospital, the children's home . . . or just that big family whose father was sick for so long. So much to be done if there were time and energy.

Oh, Lord, thank you for these small revelations. And for the very hurt of caring—for it, too, is divine.

"Inasmuch as you have done it unto one of the least of these, my brethren," you said, "you have done it unto me."

Let this be my gift to you at Christmas. And the most important gift I can give my family: All of us doing something for people who aren't as lucky as we are.

Christmas Dolls

Christmas is the time for dolls.

What a pleasure it is to shop for them, sew for them, or doctor them up to be worthy of Santa's visit on the Great Day. We women never truly outgrow our dolls—we only kiss them good-bye for a while and put them reluctantly away. Then when we have daughters of our own, we return to them joyously.

Dolls . . . dolls . . . childless women often open doll hospitals for the sheer pleasure of working with them. Or they collect dolls as a hobby. Perhaps all this is what makes it such fun to help set up the dolls for the annual Salvation Army doll party, which is usually held in the Department of Commerce building in Washington, D.C. The party is open to the public, and free. There are other toys and refreshments too; the children love not only the dolls but the space missiles, the punch and cookies, and Santa's huge red sleigh.

The dolls are like little girls, little people, as I unpack them and place them on the racks for display. Most of them are identical, the same rubber bodies, the same fixed, smiling, innocent round-eyed faces, but their clothes, made by clubs and churches throughout the area, give them identity and personality. Here are twins, in pink crocheted sweaters and bonnets. Here a saucy sailor. And now and then a sleek fashion model in earrings and a smart hairdo and a fur wrap. Or a skinny girl who is different altogether.

I come upon one such—wearing a red plaid suit and an impudent little red beret. She has a bold yet rather defensive look, as if she feels out of place among all the chubby, blandly smiling others. She is a rebel child and my heart goes out to her. I tip her head a bit forward, arrange her arms wider in a friendlier gesture, and set her spank up front, where, behold, she is the leader! A veritable cheerleader of a doll, inviting all to come and see her gay aggregation. She has come alive, she has found her place in this wonderful doll world.

People passing through the auditorium pause in puzzlement to ask what it's all about? Some of the men ask if the dolls are for sale, and I visualize the little girls at home they'd like to surprise. But I explain that no, these are here to be admired and judged for a day, then they will go to the Salvation Army Toy Center, to be distributed to needy children, and their faces go soft and pleased. They nod in agreement. They compliment the workers. They whistle softly at the size of the undertaking. And one man, strolling through, a visitor from Madison, Wisconsin, is so impressed that he writes down details.

"I want to tell my wife about this," he says. "Maybe we could get something like this started out there."

Working under the big electrical statistical board that is a feature of the Commerce lobby (that marvel that tallies births and deaths), one man comes up, eyes twinkling. Gesturing to the board, then to the vast bevy of babies, he asks, "Hey, what're you trying to do, contribute to the population explosion?"

"No," I laughed. "Just trying to make sure every little girl who wants a doll gets one Christmas morning!"

Give It to Somebody Who Needs It

There's nobody quite like a son. . . .

A certain mother in Virginia made the usual request of her children: "Now please make out your Christmas lists so your father and I can start shopping. We have to know what you want."

In a day or so the lists were presented, filled with the inevitable requests for expensive things. One message surprised them, however. It was in the form of a note from their seventeen-year-old son: "This year please take the money you would ordinarily spend on me and give it to some poor family or institution that helps kids," he asked.

"Oh, boy, here we go, he's coming down with hippieitis," they thought. And told each other, "That's out of the question; it would be too awful, everybody else opening presents Christmas morning and him without anything to unwrap."

But when they confronted their son, he explained: "Well, every time I ask for something you say, 'But that costs sixty dollars,' or 'That costs one hundred dollars.' Sure, I generally get it, but first I've got to be told how much it cost and maybe that's a good thing. Because I don't really need anything and I can't think of anything I really want. So why not take all the money you'd spend on me just because it's Christmas, and give it to somebody who does need and want things?"

As they gazed at him they realized he was serious. He preferred the warm and wonderful knowledge that somewhere, other needier kids were getting the gifts that would only be superfluous to him.

By not giving their son packages to open on Christmas morning, they would be giving him something far more valuable than they could ever buy in a store.

Let's Enjoy Christmas Together

Apron-pocket philosophy . . .

Malcolm Boyd says there is an irony in the word *apartment*. For it describes a place where people live in close proximity yet apart from each other. How sad this is. How unnecessary. An apartment ought to be a place where your opportunities for human contact multiply. Where you become friends with the janitor, the switchboard operator, meet people on the elevators, become as fond of your neighbors along the hall as you would of those down the street.

Too many people move into apartments with the fixed idea that there is some unwritten rule that you must ignore other people because they prefer it that way. Meanwhile, they deplore the fact that "nobody cares what happens to you." . . . At the same time, the people next door may be deploring this selfsame indifference in you.

Yet this rule is broken all the time. Sometimes by souls like Truman Capote's Holly Golightly, whose brash intrusions brought all kinds of joy, as well as complications, to the people in her building. Sometimes by individuals determined to break the sad prison of isolation.

A friend who occupies a plush penthouse was dreading a lonely Christmas until she decided to give a party for the faceless strangers behind all those numbers along the corridor. Feeling almost like an intruder, she slipped the invitations under their doors. To her amazement, her phone began to ring, and everybody came, rejoicing. And at the height of festivities, someone suggested, "Why don't you all come to our place for Christmas?"

Others took turns, and soon getting together for the holidays became a tradition.

Actually, there is nothing new about the demonstration of human fellowship, whether in a beehive or on the ground. In younger years we lived in numerous apartments, and nowhere did we lack for friends. Always there was some convivial soul who drew us in, or our own native need and expectations broke down barriers.

True, some people are private souls by nature. They prefer to keep to themselves, wherever they live. And people who live in apartments are often transient; knowing they *must* part by moving on, they sometimes guard against close attachments.

But then, people in neighborhoods part, too, when husbands are transferred or the house no longer serves the family's needs. So it seems a pity, with life so short and friends so sweet, to live in a state of "apart-ment," no matter where you are.

Especially at the very heart of this joyful season!

Share Your Christmas Party

To me nothing is quite so pointless, or less in keeping with the true spirit of Christmas, than gift exchanges between adults at holiday parties.

Sometimes you draw a name to buy for. Or you simply bring a wrapped gift to the affair. In either case, you find yourself frantically trying to find something besides the trite coasters, ashtrays, gags, or gimmicks within the specified price range. Then, in some annoyance, wrapping it . . . And finally—oh, goody!—making bright noises of expectation, it is your turn to accept the "surprise" of another ashtray, candy dish, gag or gimmick from a jolly ho-hoing Santa Claus.

All this on the part of grown-ups, while all over the world—yes, in your own community—children are hungry, are cold, are watching with that wide-eyed wonder and faith of children for a Santa Claus that may never come.

How can we *do* it? I wonder. How can we bear it—to spend all this money so vainly on ourselves as long as there is one youngster in our community who may wake up to an empty stocking? If we're going to buy presents at all, wouldn't it make more sense to bring them for such children? Not only more rewarding, but more fun.

A number of groups are following this course, thank goodness. With some novel ideas which add interest to the event. A friend who works for a large company told me: "Last year we had a new boss who suggested that each of us bring to our office party something we very much wanted when we were small, or in our early teens. They were wrapped as gifts and drawn, at which time each donor explained the significance of what he had brought. His first roller skates; a doll like the one she never got; a pen and pencil set. It was wonderful! We laughed and cried. The gifts were then rewrapped and divided, half sent to the Salvation Army, half to Children's Hospital. It made us all feel so good that we're doing it again this year."

Another example, a woman's club, which had a shower one year for a foundling home. "Our group of thirty women were wasting fifty or sixty dollars on knickknacks," said its president, "which we decided could be better spent on babies. So we bought blankets, crib sheets, diapers, and other things needed by the home. After all, Christ was a baby, and a needy one at that. The party had an entirely new significance for us."

The following year they contacted a home for older children, where they learned that many of the children brought there own nothing but the clothes on their backs. "We decided they might appreciate something personal, even private. So our committee has assembled boxes, which the members are covering with gaily patterned contact paper, and filling with those small items which mean so much to a boy or girl—his own ball-point pen and stationery, a bracelet, a toothbrush, a scarf, a little spending money. And to make each kit box even more personal, affixing a nameplate where each child can write his name."

Every city is full of agencies dealing with

children who need our help. Let them share your Christmas party. It will be the best one you ever had!

"Come Home with Me for Coffee"

It's fun to be a woman when . . .

You leave the chaos of cookie baking to wash the baby's face, stuff him into wraps, and changing to lipstick and heels yourself, dash off to the school program . . .

Carrying him through a chorus of angels and grinning, bathrobed Wise Men, you make your way into the auditorium, where in the back rows await the familiar faithfuls who always come.

"Here, I can see better," someone says as you sit down, "let me hold him on my lap." . . . Children in the rows ahead beam fondly on the baby and giggle when, spying a brother, he screeches his name and claps. . . . A woman seated behind you leans forward and gives you a cookie for him when he begins to fret . . .

There is the nostalgic scent of pine branches mingling with that of crayons, books and chalk. A radiator hisses. The children's voices rise shrill and sweet in the ancient carols that take you back . . . back.

"Come home with me for coffee," you impulsively invite your neighbors—and a dear friend whom you haven't seen in weeks. "The house is a mess but it'll be fun to talk."

A light snow is falling as you emerge. It makes a frail dusting on the porch and has already softly furred the handlebars of a bicycle standing at the steps. "Looks like we may have a white Christmas!" people exclaim.

The house looks tumbled but inviting as they cheerfully shed their wraps. The fragrance of your baking makes them sniff. "What smells so good?" they ask. Snatching at papers and tops, you put the kettle on, while a friend starts a fire in the fireplace.

It is going merrily by the time you return with your favorite tulip-yellow cups and the squat little Dutch pot. Like a loquacious woman itself, the fire joins the laughter and the conversation, snapping and crackling in a bright shout. . . .

You dart onto the porch to get another log. . . . The snow still falls. . . . Bright-clad children coming home from school cavort and dance in delight, holding out their arms to catch it, some of them stretching out their tongues to taste. . . .

Inside are the sounds of your friends. The cookies are crisp and rich, the coffee strong and hot.

Christmas makes being a woman fun.

A Physician Friend

A physician friend of ours who works wonders with disturbed children often gives a Christmas party for his patients, at which he reads aloud Dickens' *Christmas Carol*. Last year, however, he had scarcely started on the adventures of Scrooge, when his audience protested, "Aaaw, we saw all this the other night on Mr. Magoo!"

"Lionel Barrymore I could take," he mourns. "But boy, to have to play second fiddle to Mr. Magoo!"

Part 2

Celebration

Chapter 5

THE CHRISTMAS STAR

And Lo, the Star!

And lo, the star, which they saw in the east, went before them, until it came and stood over where the young child was. (Matthew 2:9)

 ur destiny, they say, is written in the stars.

And looking back, I seem to see my childhood and early years through a sparkling array of stars, both real and symbolic.

"Star light, star bright, first star I've seen tonight," we'd chant at dusk, and make our magic wishes. And as more stars came peeping out as if to watch, we'd play our wild chasing games of Hide and Go Seek or Run, Sheep, Run! beneath their fairy light. For in Storm Lake, Iowa, where I was raised, the skies are a vast open meadow. On summer nights the stars bloom in fiery profusion, like flowers or silver cockleburs. Sometimes they seemed so close you could almost reach up and pluck one. In winter the bare trees wear them like jewels on their fingers.

My family were all stargazers. Like David, we often stretched out on the sweet-smelling grass at bedtime to watch the stars. Or we would walk the weedy path to the old wooden dock on the lake. This was even better, because the water multiplied their brilliance, and when the wind stirred, combed them through its dark hair.

Oh, the cool, damp, fishy smell of that slightly swaying dock as we cuddled down under the blanket Dad had brought. It was wrapped around Mother, but we crept inside, nuzzling like ponies vying to be close, while our parents pointed out planets and told us stories of the stars.

Venus. Mars. The Milky Way splashing its foamy brilliance. "That's because the Big Dipper spilled the milk," Dad said, "and the Great Bear—see him up there?—is trying to lap it up." Mother tried to find the constellation named for a lovely maiden, Andromeda. "The Greek hero Perseus rescued her from a sea monster and put her in the sky."

We shivered and huddled closer. "Are there monsters in the lake?"

"No, honey. Besides, it's just a myth."

"I see the Great Bear and the middle-size bear and the little bear and Goldilocks!" a sister claimed. "Is the Three Bears a constellation?"

"It can be yours," Mother said in spite of our laughter. "That's how the constellations got their names in the first place. People found pictures in the stars and made up stories to fit them. You can see anything you want to in the stars."

See anything you want to . . . *or be whatever you want to,* if you just look at the stars. For there is in each of us a childlike hunger for recognition, achievement, rewards. And the best symbol the world has been able to come up with is a star.

At Sunday School we sang "Will There Be Any Stars in My Crown?" And at public school worked eagerly for those little gold stars teachers might put on our papers. As even today big tough college football teams wear stars on their helmets for outstanding plays.

At school too, we saluted the flag every morning. The Stars and Stripes. And we were taught its origin. Those were the days of patriotism and pride. Every child had his own little cloth flag on a stick to wave and carry. And no concert, speech or public gathering ever began without pledging allegiance, or closed without the whole crowd standing and singing "The Star-Spangled Banner." Oh, but it was a flag to look up to in those days, our flag with its stars.

To look up . . . toward the stars. The very lexicon of our elders urging us to better ourselves was replete with stars. "Hitch your wagon to a star," advised parents and teachers. And, "If you would hit the trees, shoot for the stars." There were also people to look up to—great men like Charles Lindbergh, who actually soared from the earth to fly across the ocean among the stars. And oh, how we worshiped our movie stars!

No, the stars weren't all overhead. Yet, winter and summer the broad Iowa skies did arch our lives, and when night fell we never failed to notice the lovely stars.

But the star that meant the most to us as children was the Christmas star. We began watching for it a week or two before the holiday, and vied to be the first to spy its brilliance. For always it seemed there was one star in the East whose size and beauty outshone all the rest. With the same zeal we competed to see who could fashion the best cardboard silver star to crown our Christmas tree.

The tree was usually a tall fragrant prickly fir cut from Uncle Harrison's farm. Our uncle would deliver it—a big noisy ruddy man as jovial as Santa Claus in his boots and stocking cap and shaggy raccoon coat. And to hear his bobsled with its jingling bells coming down the street was almost as exciting as a visit from the jolly elf himself. After much stamping and shaking and brushing off of snow, the tree would be hauled in and set up before the big bay window, not quite touching the ceiling, so as to leave room for the winning star.

Mother would have already brought down from the attic her faithful box of decorations. Collapsible paper bells rustled as they danced above the hot air register. Ropes of red and green garlanded the doors. There were strings of tarnished tinsel and a few precious ornaments, fragile as robin's eggs in their nests of tissue paper. These we unwrapped and hung on the tree with care. But the really serious business would go on after supper, for no tree was properly trimmed without our handiwork.

When the dishes were cleared, we knelt on chairs around the round oak table, scribbling and whacking and pasting joyously away. First, the chains made out of links of thick construction paper, and stuck with flour and water paste. Though sometimes (ah, luxury) there was a bottle of library paste, new and sweet-smelling from the drugstore.

Meanwhile, the merry rattling and heavenly scent of popcorn floated from the kitchen. Mother dumped it into a dishpan and brought it to us for stringing. Dad, squinting, would thread the needles and show us how to pierce the delicate white blossoms. Though their flesh was so frail that no matter how careful you were, the kernels would break. Cranberries were easier; the needle plunged through their scarlet hearts with juicy pops, and soon you had a bright necklace for a branch of the patiently waiting tree.

Somehow, by common consent all this must be accomplished before we even started our stars. For stars were tricky too. It is hard to draw a perfect star. But fat, skinny or lopsided, we cut them out of cardboard and covered them with shiny tinfoil stripped from gum wrappers or candy bars. Then from the cluttered silvery firmament of our efforts, Dad would choose the best.

"Golly, they're all so pretty, I can't decide!" he'd claim, scratching his bald head. And he'd circle the table round and round, lifting and studying each one while your heart raced. Finally he'd end the suspense. "The winner!" he'd announce, holding the largest, least crooked one high. Then, with a bow and a flourish, he would lead its beaming creator to the stepladder, steady his climb to the ceiling, and aid with the careful hanging of the star. Only when that homemade silver star reigned secure could the tiny candles be lit.

And lo, the star signaled that Christmas had truly begun!

Stars shine through the whole beautiful story of Christmas Eve. Shepherds watching their flocks on a frosty hillside, when out of the starry heavens angels appeared, proclaiming the glorious news. And the Wise Men who journeyed so long and far, guided only by the great and brilliant star.

And lo, the star, which they saw in the east, went before them, until it came and stood over where the young child was.

We saw it, we saw it! Of course we saw it, walking to church with our parents through the sparkling snow. And like those Wise Men we rejoiced "with exceeding great joy." There were stars everywhere on that blessed night. Explosions of tiny stars under the corner street-lights, the very walks and drifts. There were stars in people's voices calling, "Merry Christmas!" And after the pageant and the carols, stars in children's eyes rushing home to hang up stockings, or to lie quivering, listening for the beat of tiny hooves.

Oh, stars will always be special for Christmas. And stars don't change.

But we all need stars to brighten our lives every day of the year. Stars to wish on, stars to mark our achievements. Though we outgrow those little gold stars on school papers, we're never too big for the stars of a compliment, a word of appreciation, an honor, an award.

And how we need stars to shoot for, stars to steer by. A faith, a program, a goal on which to fix the course of our lives. And for this we need stars we can look up to, people who can inspire us, lead us. This we need most of all, especially when we are young.

Sadly, in this loud, violent, drug- and sex-oriented era, many of the stars our children worship are antiheroes. Sometimes they seem little more than painted demons with amplifiers. Where have all the heroes gone? we sometimes wonder. Where, oh, where are all the stars?

Then we remember that we already have a hero who lives beyond time and place. The star of the Christmas story. Not just the pretty baby in the manger, but a great and mighty man who walked the roads healing the sick, restoring sight to the blind. Teaching mercy, love, forgiveness, yet rousing the people to injustice. A man who wasn't afraid to denounce the leaders of his country as whited sepulchers and hypocrites. A man who took up a whip and lashed the crooked moneychangers from the Temple.

A man willing to die for his convictions.

I believe he was indeed the long-awaited Messiah, son of God. But even those who don't, acknowledge that he was a star of genuine magnitude. Yet that he was no legend, he actually lived, and no life ever so profoundly affected the world. And despite all the commercialism and hedonism today, lo, that star still shines!

Multitudes, young and old, still follow him. To many of the young he *is* literally *Jesus Christ Superstar*. Some found him during the very time of chaos when that Broadway musical was written. Many were healed of drug addiction, others were led into lives of service. Others found him in different ways, or never lost sight of him at all. Go to church this Christmas Eve and you will see young people there, often with little new families of their own.

They probably didn't walk to church as we did, crunching through the sparkling snow. And the star that shines atop their tree probably wasn't fashioned by eager fingers out of cardboard and tinfoil. But surely the loving excitement was just as great when it was hung. And going and coming, I'm sure they scanned the skies, just as we did, searching among its jewels for one brighter than all the rest—the beautiful Christmas star.

Christmas Bells of Bethlehem

There is a beautiful custom in England, instituted by the British Broadcasting Company. On Christmas morning they start ringing bells from different parishes throughout the Empire, and finish with the ringing of the bell of the Church of the Nativity in Bethlehem.

I visited this holy city one summer, birthplace of King David and of the Christ Child. It is only a few miles south of Jerusalem, a town of some 20,000, mostly Christians. Yet its famous church is guarded by Israeli soldiers.

Bethlehem means "house of meat" (*beit lahm*) in Arabic, and "house of bread" (*beit lehem*) in Hebrew. A basilica of the Nativity was erected by Constantine in the fourth century at the site of the famous inn, with its underground stables. It was transformed by Justinian in the sixth century, and escaped Persian destruction in 614 because the invaders recognized their national costume, worn by the Magi (or Wise Men) represented on a mosaic.

Destroyed and restored many times, the church is now built in the shape of a cross, and is administered by Greek and Armenian Orthodox Christians. It is very beautiful indeed, especially the grotto, traditional site of the manger.

There were not many tourists during that hot month of August, perhaps partly because people were fearful of the hostilities between Arabs and Jews. But a sense of great peace and reverence prevailed, certainly a gentle respect among the Israeli soldiers. And there was something both kind and paradoxical about their execution of a certain duty: To inform women about to enter this Christian shrine that they must wear skirts instead of shorts, and cover their arms.

And on Christmas day each year the bells at that holy site, as well as bells all over England, ring out peace on earth and good will to all!

Chapter 6

CHRISTMAS TODAY
AND YESTERDAY

*Wrapping Presents
in the Good Old Days*

D ialogue with a young wrapping assistant . . .

"How did you wrap packages in the olden days, Mother? Before they had Scotch tape?"

My goodness, how *did* we manage? But, you hasten to correct, "See here, it wasn't exactly the olden days. Why, sticky tape's been on the market something like"—you hazard a guess—"maybe thirty years."

To an eight-year-old, however, you realize that such a figure equals an epoch. "Okay, in the olden days we didn't have so much fancy paper, either. Mostly we used plain white tissue paper and stuck it together with gay little seals like these."

"Hey, white tissue paper? If you wanted to peek at what you got, that'd be great!"

"Tell me some more!" he begs.

"Well, the packages did look pretty with all these little seals that you can hardly see on all this fancy paper that we have today. We children licked the seals for those we were wrapping, and made our own patterns sticking them on."

"Didn't you have any fancy paper at all?"

"Oh, a little. Some with green trees on it, or holly, or red Santas. But gradually the elegant papers began to be printed.

"And when people sent us packages wrapped in it, we could simply pick the seals off and smooth it out and save it for our own packages the next year."

"I like to save real pretty paper too," he says. "But it always gets torn where they put the tape."

"That's the trouble with these modern inventions," you laugh. "For everything you gain, there's something you lose.

"So hand me that paper with the pink angels trimming the golden tree on it—and while you're at it, a roll of Scotch tape."

Wouldn't You Like a Dime Every Time?

You have absolutely sworn to get your shopping done early, with every out-of-town package on its way by Thanksgiving, or at least by those deadlines the post office is always setting—only to find yourself straggling in at the last minute and sending things Priority Mail or Express Mail to get them there on time.

The Old-fashioned Catalog

"Look, children, see what's come in the mail," I summoned my young one day. "A big fat mail order catalog!"

They rushed up to see what I was so pleased about. And reacted with about as much enthusiasm as if I'd just presented them with a big fat telephone directory. Its plethora of riches failed to impress them; they see all this and more in store windows every day. And whoever heard of sending away for something you haven't both seen and been fervently exhorted to buy on TV? Politely, they listen to my promises that when it got a little older I'd let them cut it up for paper dolls—and escaped.

Somewhat saddened, I stood sniffing its elusive, nostalgic scent of thin inky pages and thick glossy ones, letting myself be whisked back to the days when the arrival of mail order catalogs signaled spring and fall. Like spying your first robin, or a scarlet maple leaf. *Sears Roebuck. Montgomery Ward.* What magical names! For if you lived in a small town or out in the country, they brought the whole thrilling world to your door.

This was important in several ways. For those often snowbound, without much choice of merchandise in the few available stores, these vast packages of print and pictures spread before dazzled eyes almost everything known to the needs of man. Entire families were often clothed and outfitted from their pages. Whole houses were furnished by mail—curtains, rugs, parlor set, nickel-plated stove, and even the kitchen sink. But more, the catalog was a source of information, of contact, a glimpse of fabulous people at work and play. It was a springboard for hope, the touchstone of dreams.

To children, its arrival was as if Santa Claus himself had walked in the door. We fought over turns to explore it, lying enrapt on the floor. We spent hours poring over its pages, especially before Christmas, greedily drawing up long impossible lists from the section marked Toys. Desperately though we yearned, fervently though we believed in the miracle of possessing, I don't think it was the *getting* that really mattered. In these orgies of imagination we were fulfilled.

In the same way we spent thousands of nonexistent dollars fervently filling out discarded blanks as we "ordered" the most expensive items—furniture, jewelry, furs.

Most important of all were the paper dolls. With the advent of a new catalog we were free to race for the scissors and start cutting up the old. Having each chosen a basic beauty, we would then whack off the heads and feet of other models in order to equip her with a wardrobe worthy of a queen. True, the arms were often in curious positions and the garments didn't always fit; no matter, the dolls continued to beam and that was good enough for us.

Again, we would choose someone we wanted to be. Gloria Swanson, Aunt Tressa, the minister, the mayor, a town belle—and hunt until we found a fancied likeness. We then cut out families for them—dolls that suited and matched their real or imagined circles. My brother dubbed these our "Hippity People"— perhaps because of the way they danced across the floor in a breeze or a blast from the hot-air furnace. Each of us picked a corner of the dining room, where we set up housekeeping with our chosen family.

They became vitally real to us one long cold winter when we were housebound with a succession of measles, mumps, and chicken pox. Gloria Swanson visited back and forth with Uncle Horace, the minister, the judge's family. Their children went to parties and dances, had weddings, and when one of them got torn in two, had a funeral. (We found everything in the catalog but the casket.) Then one day when the snow was melting, my brother took the lot of them outside for a boat ride. He was gone a long time. Returning, he confessed. The boat had upset and all our Hippity People were drowned. We all cried. Somehow, it spelled the end of our catalog paper dolls. And the beginning of our growing up.

Yet we never outgrew our awed admiration for the beautiful creatures in those books. What grace they had—standing hand on hip as they chatted with each other—what charm, what style. On them even a housedress looked enticing. And the men were so suave and handsome, they glorified even a pair of Big Huck overalls. In the never-never land they inhabited there was no dirt, no dishwater, no floors to scrub, no spilled oatmeal. Everyone was radiant, young, enchanting, and it seemed that if only you could obtain their garments for yourself or your parents, somehow your own dull, small everyday world would become enchanting as well. How was it possible to believe otherwise, especially when you read the poetic prose in which they were described?

Though Mother, too, faithfully studied and loved her catalogs, she seldom sent away for things. "It's hard to tell how things really look from a picture," she said. "And besides, you can't always be sure they'll fit. Also," she reasoned, "we should support our hometown merchants. They've been good to us." ("Good to us" meant letting us have credit when times were hard.) We found her attitude frustrating in view of this surefire magic. She didn't have many clothes, and my sister and I longed to send away and get her a dress.

A dress was simply beyond our means, after weeks of saving, so we decided to settle for a hat. We picked out the prettiest we could find, not a very big hat, but one richly adorned with fruit and flowers. Eagerly we filled out the order blank, stealthily emptying our banks and slipping off to the post office to buy a money order. We could hardly wait. We wanted it in time for Easter. Our suspense was agonizing as the weeks slipped by. Every time she longingly fingered a hat downtown, or spoke about trimming an old one, we were tempted to tell her.

At last the mail truck stopped before our house. As the driver marched up the walk and knocked, we thought we would explode. "But we didn't order anything," Mother protested, even as we began to shout: "Surprise! Surprise!" Baffled, she opened the box, lifted the hat out of the tissue paper, and there it was in all its glory. Even more gorgeous than we had imagined, rosy and shiny, velvet-ribboned, it was a veritable cornucopia of fruit and flowers.

"Oh, my!" Mother exclaimed, looking slightly dismayed. She picked it up gingerly, turning it around on her hand. "This is for *me?*" She'd never worn anything but the plainest of hats; obviously she was almost too overcome with joy to speak.

She went at once to the mirror and put it on, with some difficulty, over her generous mounds of hair. Her hair was her crowning glory. The hat sort of rode on back of it like a ship perched upon a wave. Until that moment it had never occurred to us that the hat might not become her. In our loving dreams she would be transformed before our eyes into a likeness of one of those dream creatures of the catalog.

Instead, Mother turned to us, looking stricken—half sad, half amused. "Oh, girls, girls, it's the most beautiful hat in the world!" she cried, embracing us. "Just wait, I'll curl my hair Saturday night and Sunday I'll have my powder on. It'll look just—fine!"

It did. It almost did. We all complimented her profusely when she was ready for church, and so did her friends when she got there. But something was wrong and we knew it with a queer wrench in the region of our stomachs. It was our first troubled sip of that wry brew, disillusionment. I think we grew up a little that day, as we had on the death of our paper dolls.

Mother loyally wore the hat—how long I don't recall. After a while it didn't look funny on her anymore, it simply became a part of her, like her dependable blue crepe dress. When its flowers began to wilt, its fruit to wither, she even doctored them up and wore it some more. She was actually regretful when at last she was forced to abandon it. "I'll never forget this hat," she said, and she spoke for all of us.

I think of it now on that rare occasion when a catalog comes in the mail. I thought of it as I tried to rouse in my children the sense of delight that a catalog used to bring. But a catalog cannot be the passport to wonder to them that it was to us. These children who are so rich in material things that they are desperately poor in the need for make-believe.

No, really to thrill to the magic of a catalog you must live in the country or a little town. And be a pigtailed dreamer in the days when winters were long and lonely . . . and paper dolls came alive, and a hat was truly a Hat to be worn lengthily, head high, by a mother who loved her little girls.

The Secret of the Christmas Tree

There is no more beautiful celebration of Christmas than in that great city which belongs to all of us, Washington, D.C. Each year a different state ships to the nation's capital its tallest, most magnificent tree. This is erected on the mall, as the crowning feature of the Pageant of Peace. I have stood there with my children awaiting the thrilling moment when, at the touch of the President's hand, that tree springs into fabulous, living light.

We have sat in the National Cathedral, hearing choirs of trained voices present Handel's *Messiah*. We have walked the fairyland of lighted streets. We have gazed into the marvels of animation in store windows, depicting the legends and fantasies of the holiday. On rare occasions when the weather was cold enough, our sons have joined the ice skaters who skim below Lincoln's feet on the famous Reflecting Pool. We have toured the White House decked out in all its festive attire; all the skills of professional artists and decorators combine to achieve perfection in this perfect mansion for this perfect holiday.

But we have always stood longest in the foyer where, usually, there stands an old-fashioned, ceiling-high, popcorn- and cookie-trimmed Christmas tree. There are gingerbread men too, and quaint and fragile ornaments. There are nuts and fruits and velvet bows such as a mother might have kept in her dresser drawer. There are chains of paper loops like children used to make.

And this, it seems to me, is significant. That in a land of sophistication and plenty, the truest symbol of Christmas is, after all, an old-fashioned family kind of tree.

It brings back all the Christmases past that I knew as a little girl. It brings back the winter sports that were their glorious preview: the ice skating, the snow battles, the hopping of bobs. An entire new era of delight was ushered in with the first snowfall, and with the freezing of the lake it became an intense reality.

The lake, that vast rolling body of water in which we had frolicked like savages all summer, became forbidden territory soon after Labor Day. Though it continued to rush shoreward with foaming force, we knew that the days of its might were numbered. Winter was watching from behind the gold, then gradually naked, trees. Soon the water would lie subdued, the first sheets of ice inching out from the shore. Every day some daring boy would test its surface, racing back at the sounds of cracking. But the cold and certain encroachment was taking place; until one day, after severe nights and several false reports, the word would race through town: "The lake's frozen over!" And though parents remained doubtful and issued edicts and warnings, the first few figures began taking tentative swings across its glassy expanse.

"Darn fools," our dad would declare. "You kids aren't setting foot on that ice until we're sure it's safe."

"But it is!" we'd claim. "Old Doc Vanderhoof's been going out every day."

Old Vanderhoof, a retired "horse doctor," was also our local Hans Brinker. Dutch-born, a superb skater. Whenever you saw that tubby figure, arms folded, pipe in his mouth, white whiskers blowing, doing his loops and turns, the parents were assured. The ice was safe.

Our skates had been ready for days. Dug from cellar, barn or attic, sharpened, polished, their worn straps tested, tried on repeatedly. "Now take those things off," Mother scolded, as we clumped or wobbled about. "You'll cut the rug and you'll scar the floor." Each year we inherited bigger ones from older brothers and sisters, and passed ours down. Or you traded with the neighbors. Sometimes the purchase of a new pair was not to be avoided, and, oh, the thrill of those tough, strong, leathery-smelling straps, the brilliance of the blades. Shoe skates were unheard of. It was important, therefore, to have strong, thick-soled shoes for the clamps to clutch.

Once, for my birthday in late September, I asked only for my own brand-new ice skates. They seemed unbearably beautiful lying in the box. I'd test their sharpness with a finger, and sometimes, in secret, hold their cold promise against my cheek. The weather seemed unseasonably warm, the wait for their initiation intolerable. Worse, the high-top black shoes with which they were to be worn were getting thin. By the time the ice and the lovely skates were ready, the shoes were shot. It was a lean year, and new ones were out of the question. I had to suffer the ignominy, after all, of some beaten-up old straps across the toes.

We lived only two blocks from the lake. On Saturdays, and most days after school, we hastened down to The Point, a favorite gathering place. Here a tipsy old green boathouse afforded shelter from the stinging blasts. It was always intensely cold, and though we were lumpy with long underwear and bundled to the eyebrows in layers of sweaters, jackets, leggings, mufflers, and mittens, we huddled in its protection, or drew gratefully toward the great crackling fire that older boys often built among the rocks.

Armed with stubby brooms, the boys would have swept the snow aside for a hockey court. And what blithe young gods they seemed as they smacked the little puck with their store-bought or homemade hockey sticks, laughing, yelling, fighting with a fierce and joyous abandon; or often gliding swiftly up to see how the girls were getting along.

There was about them a gallantry and kindness absolutely singular to this contact. At home or at school they might ignore us, tease us, pull our hair or even hit us, but at this gathering upon the ice they became knights in stocking caps and mackinaws. They helped us with our skates; they asked if we were warm enough, and if we weren't, they made us go home or sometimes rubbed our hands and feet. They taught the beginners patiently; they steered us about, showing us figure eights and how to skate backward, and other fancy tricks. And no matter who it was, even a brother or some dumb neighbor kid, a sense of our own fledgling womanhood was sweetly roused by their attentiveness. While to have one of the true heroes, say a football player or a town lifeguard, kneel at your feet just to tighten a skate was to fall instantly, madly, hopelessly in love.

The boys never suffered us to join their hockey games. And, true Vikings that they were, girls had no place on their iceboats. They fashioned these magical craft themselves out of two-by-fours hauled home from the lumberyard by sled or coaster wagon. These they nailed together crosswise and masted with a piece of canvas, or more likely a mother's bedsheet. The runners and rudders they carved of wood, the runners bladed with strips of metal which were forged and shaped to their purpose by Pat McCabe in his blacksmith shop. We sometimes watched the process, Pat's white teeth flashing in his smoke-blackened face. The glow of his forge lit up the mysterious recesses of his cavern where all manner of interesting objects hung: wagon wheels and horseshoes, pipes and bars and farming tools. There was the smell of hot iron and horses and leather and steam as this skilled and dusky wizard plied his trade.

Perched at front or rear of the boats, or lying flat, the boys steered these fleet ships into vast blue gleaming distances of the lake where only a foolhardy skater dared venture. (There were air holes; every now and then the town was shaken by some skater's shooting into such a hole and being trapped beneath the ice. This was our parents' greatest concern.) But the iceboaters were charmed beings, winged by the wind, flying safe and free.

Boys also fought pitched battles behind their snow forts, and here the girls were allowed, if only in the capacity of providing ammunition. Our job was to make the snowballs, and we gloated over our growing stock, much as our mothers proudly counted their canning. A good snowball maker was much in demand. I always envied Gert Beatty, who was first to be chosen when she trudged out. She fashioned round, firm snowballs with the same methodical skill that she turned out loaves of bread for her mother, or a firm, creamy platter of fudge. Hers put my leaky, lopsided snowballs to shame. An even higher honor was accorded Kac Ford, a girl who knew more about football than most boys, and had such a terrific pitching arm she was not only allowed on the team, she sometimes led the charge.

Yet for sheer exhilarating delight, nothing could equal hitching bobsled rides. With the onset of winter, cars were hoisted onto blocks to protect the tires, and stored away. There were simply no facilities for sweeping the snow-muffled streets. Townspeople walked (or waded) to their destination; country people traveled by bob. Saturday was the big trading day in town, and consequently the best day for hopping bobs. Farmers approaching Storm Lake by almost any road were met by a swarm of kids, most of them pulling sleds. If you didn't have a sled, you hopped on the long wooden runner and hung on to the wagon box. With a sled you looped its rope over a bolt at the back or through a brace at its side.

A good-natured farmer usually *"Whoa-ed!"* his team to a halt so that you could get attached, or he at least slowed down. A mean one, spying the eager contingent, would whip his horses on faster. It was fun to run madly after him, trying to catch him anyway. It added to the thrill. Hooking a ride with someone who didn't even suspect you were there was especially exciting, dangerous as it was. He might make a sudden turn or stop and throw you off.

Parents were always issuing futile edicts against the hopping of bobs. Yet they, too, remembered the thrill of lying belly-flat upon a sled that went whistling and bouncing across the crusty and glittering ground—here bumpy, here glass-smooth, here stained mustard-yellow, here grayly tramped, here purest shining white . . . while up front there was the steady plocking rhythm of the horses' hooves, the jingle of harness, the creak and rattle of the wagon box, while sometimes wisps of straw flew back like pinfeathers from angel wings.

Clutching the wooden rudders of our sleds; we steered, avoiding the deeper ruts; and rounding a corner, trying not to swing too far to the side. You could lose your grip, skid off, hit a curb, a lamppost, or be hurled into the path of an oncoming team. Thus the perils, tempering our pleasure, yet enhancing it.

Bobsleds were great to ride in, too, out to Grandpa Holmes' or an uncle's, snuggled down on the tickling straw. We made tents of the scratchy, raw-smelling horse blankets, and burrowed down like groundhogs, cozy and squirming, with sometimes a heated soapstone or a hot, carpet-wrapped brick at our feet. We played pioneer—we were crouched in a covered wagon, and the amiable small-town sounds beyond or the whistling wind of the open country were the threatening howls of wolves or Indians.

Even Santa Claus came by bobsled. A couple of weeks before Christmas his impending arrival was proclaimed by the businessmen. Everybody gathered downtown, kids shoving and falling off the curbs in frantic anticipation. Then came the sweet, familiar jangling of his sleigh bells, and there was the old boy himself, waving a mittened paw and tossing out bags of candy while some assistant drove the team.

A free show at the movie followed. "To get us kids out of the way so our folks can buy our presents," smart-alecky older ones claimed. We were doubtful and stricken. But we'd just seen him. "Aaah, that was just ol' Matt McDermott dressed up," hooted the heretics sitting behind. And they jiggled the musty velour seat. "We peeked through the courthouse window and seen him stuffing a pillow down his pants!" It was too funny, and too awful to believe. Yet it didn't really matter. Sucking blissfully on the hard painted candies, watching Tom Mix or Harold Lloyd, we were content in the awareness of some loving adult conspiracy on our behalf.

The fantasy of Santa Claus seemed not in the least at odds with the mail order catalogs over which we crouched, making long, drunken lists that had to be whittled down to plausible proportions. Nor with the noisy bedlam of shopping in our little stores. Nor with the hum of Mother's sewing machine at night. Over and over we'd ask, "What for?" if only to hear the beloved reply: "What fur? Cat fur to make kitten britches!" Pressed, she might admit that she was helping Santa's elves. "He's not going to be able to do as much as he'd like to this year." Then, among the few new toys of Christmas morning we would find bean bags, doll clothes, little cloth purses for Sunday School.

The old pine chest in the storeroom held all sorts of oddments from which she drew: scraps of flannel left over from diapers, velvet and gingham, quilt blocks, buttons, embroidery cotton. Here she hid both her handiwork and her purchases; and it was understood by all that no one looked in the box. The most miserable Christmas I ever had was the year I yielded to temptation and found what I most desperately wanted, a real working Ouija board.

Mother exchanged gifts with a number of chums who lived elsewhere—Aunt Tressa, Aunt Anna, Aunt Mabel, as we called them. She worked openly on their presents, tatting or crocheting doilies and edgings, her shuttle dipping like a little fat bird, the dainty beak of her crochet hook plucking and pulling and picking—almost tasting the threads. She wrapped her efforts in white tissue paper, thin as new snow, and bound them with silver cords. And those rectangles of white and silver seemed in their loveliness to be jeweled blocks for the palace of the Ice Princess.

By now she would have brought forth the family decorations—rough ropes of red and green to loop above the lace curtains and garland the living room. And several paper bells, which lay flat until unfolded, when lo! they bloomed fat and full to hang in doorways and dance in the heat of the hardcoal stove. For us, as for most people, this was all. And while the churches boasted Christmas trees, they were almost unknown in private homes when I was very small.

I shall never forget our first one. Two gentle maiden ladies who lived next door called Mother over one day; and when she returned she was excitedly bearing an enormous box. Desperate for its secret, we plagued her until she yielded at least initials: C.T.D. We spent almost as much time trying to guess their meaning as learning our pieces for the Christmas Eve program at church.

This program, at first mostly songs and recitations, later a pageant, was as much a part of Christmas as hanging up your stocking. We practiced religiously, and if possible got a new dress. Snow squeaked underfoot and sparkled under the streetlights as the family walked to the church. Grandpa Griffith, who was janitor, always built a big fire early. The church was warm and spicy with the scent of the tall fir tree beside the stage. Standing over the hot-air register, we admired the way our skirts ballooned.

Sunday School teachers frantically began assembling angels in their proper rows. Shadows moved behind white sheets hung up for curtains. Garbed in bathrobes and turbaned in towels, your father and other men became strangers, saying, "Let us go now even unto Bethlehem and see this thing which has come to pass . . ." And the click and swish of the sheets being pulled—and at last the revelation: For there stood Joseph beside a manger with real straw! And Mary cradling a baby—sometimes a big doll, but once a real baby! The minister's new baby! You could hear it crowing and glimpse a flailing hand. It lived! And for a breathless, rapturous moment the living, breathing Christ Child was right there in your midst.

After the pageant there was an anxious, squirming hush in which you knew something else magical was about to happen. A jangling of sleigh bells heightened the suspense as the superintendent asked, "What's that? Do I hear

somebody?" And the wild and frenzied scream-
ing as he appeared, so big and jolly he sometimes almost knocked over the red cardboard
fireplace climbing out—"Santa, Santa Claus!"

As you grew older he began to look familiar—like Mr. Samsel or Simon Thomas, but
no matter—when he patted your head or
handed you a bag of hard candies he became
the droll elf of the eternal fairy tale of North
Pole and make-believe.

And the Ladies' Aid served cookies and
coffee, and parents visited, and children, mad
with anticipation, begged to go home lest he
miss their house. . . . And at last you all poured
out onto the steps that had been paved with
ground diamonds.

"Good night, Merry Christmas, come to
see us!" voices called as families set off along
the cold sparkling streets. The snow had usually stopped by now. The night was still and
clear. All the stars glittered. But there was always one bigger and brighter than the rest. A
great gem that seemed to stand still as if to
mark the mystery. And you gazed at it in wonder all the way home.

There you scurried for bed and lay hugging yourself, listening to the sweet lullaby of
Christmas Eve—parental voices murmuring,

the rattle of paper, the tinkle and squeak of treasures unguessed.

Awake before daylight that special Christmas, we found Mother already in the room to restrain us. "Wait!" she said. Something strange was going on. Then when a voice called, "Ready, Rose," she led us forth—into fairyland. Or so it seemed. For there in the living room bloomed a miracle: a Christmas tree! Its candles twinkled and fluttered as if hosts of butterflies and birds had alighted on its branches. From its arms gleamed dozens of fragile beads and baubles and ornaments. We stared at it, eyes shining, too dazzled to speak.

And now we knew the secret of the box, C.T.D. "Christmas Tree Decorations," Mother laughed. "The Misses Spicer had them as young ladies in Europe and want our family to have them now."

This lovely gift became the basis for all the trees that followed. We augmented it with strings of popcorn, paper chains, gilded walnuts, and later, when they were plentiful, cranberries. The exquisite fragrance (and hazard) of the tallow candles was replaced by electric bulbs, while tinsel and icicles and fine new ornaments almost crowded out those exquisite early ones. But no tree, however splendid, will be as beautiful as that first one. And no gifts, however expensive or plentiful, can surpass the joy of those precious few we found under it that day. . . .

Today Santa travels by jet or helicopter instead of bobsled or sleigh. We hear a lot about the commercial Christmas, the cocktail party instead of church on Christmas Eve. But we also have a Pageant of Peace in our nation's capital, based on the message of the Christ Child, and the eyes of the world are turned upon it as our President launches that pageant with the lighting of the national Christmas tree. While in the White House (which is your house, too, and mine) there stands a symbol of the invincible American family, an old-fashioned tree.

Thank goodness, despite all other changes, this one thing remains. It is the secret of our freedom and our greatness. It is the true secret of America, its magic and its stability. It is the secret of the Christmas tree.

Chapter 7

HOME FOR CHRISTMAS

At Christmas the Heart Goes Home

t Christmas all roads lead home.

The filled planes, packed trains, overflowing buses, all speak eloquently of a single destination: home. Despite the crowding and the crushing, the delays, the confusion, we clutch our bright packages and beam our anticipation. We are like birds driven by an instinct we only faintly understand—the hunger to be with our own people.

If we are already snug by our own fireside

surrounded by growing children, or awaiting the return of older ones who are away, then the heart takes a side trip. In memory we journey back to the Christmases of long ago. Once again we are curled into quivering balls of excitement, listening to the mysterious rustle of tissue paper and the tinkle of untold treasures as parents perform their magic on Christmas Eve. Or we recall the special Christmases that are like little landmarks in the life of a family.

One memory is particularly dear to me—a Christmas during the Great Depression when Dad was out of work and the rest of us were scattered, struggling to get through school or simply to survive. My sister Gwen and her schoolteacher husband, on his first job in another state, were expecting their first baby. My brother Harold, an aspiring actor, was traveling with a road show. I was a senior working my way through a small college five hundred miles away. My boss had offered me fifty dollars—a fortune!—just to keep the office open the two weeks he and his wife would be gone.

"And boy, do I need the money. Mom, I know you'll understand," I wrote.

I wasn't prepared for her brave if wistful reply. The other kids couldn't make it either. Except for my kid brother Barney, she and

Dad would be alone. "This house is going to seem empty, but don't worry—we'll be okay."

I did worry, though. Our first Christmas apart! And as the carols drifted up the stairs, as the corridors rang with the laughter and chatter of other girls packing up to leave, my misery deepened.

Then one night when the dorm was almost empty I had a long distance call. "Gwen!" I gasped. "What's wrong?" (Long distance usually meant an emergency back in those days.)

"Listen, Leon's got a new generator and we think the old jalopy can make it home. I've wired Harold—if he can meet us halfway, he can ride with us. But don't tell the folks; we want to surprise them. Marj, you've just got to come too."

"But I haven't got a dime for presents."

"Neither have we. Cut up a catalog and bring pictures of all the goodies you'd buy if you could—and will someday!"

"I could do *that,* Gwen. But I just can't leave here now."

When we hung up I reached for the scissors. Furs and perfume. Wristwatches, clothes, cars—how all of us longed to lavish beautiful things on those we loved. Well, at least I could mail mine home—with IOUs.

I was still dreaming over this "wish list" when I was called to the phone again. It was my boss, saying he'd decided to close the office after all. My heart leaped up, for if it wasn't too late to catch a ride as far as Fort Dodge with the girl down the hall . . . ! I ran to pound on her door.

They already had a load, she said—but if I was willing to sit on somebody's lap . . . Her dad was downstairs waiting. I threw things into a suitcase, then rammed a hand down the torn lining of my coat sleeve so fast it emerged mittened and I had to start over.

It was snowing as we piled into that heaterless car. We drove all night with the side curtains flapping, singing and hugging each other to keep warm. Not minding—how could we? We were going home! . . .

"Marj!" Mother stood at the door, clutching her robe about her, silver-black hair spilling down her back, eyes large with alarm, then incredulous joy. "Oh . . . *Marj*."

I'll never forget those eyes or the feel of her arms around me, so soft and warm after the bitter cold. My feet felt frozen after that all-night drive, but they warmed up as my parents fed me and put me to bed. And when I woke up hours later, it was to the jangle of the sleigh bells Dad hung on the door each year. And voices. My kid brother shouting, "Harold! Gwen!" The clamor of astonished greetings, the laughter, the kissing, the questions. And we all gathered around the kitchen table the way we used to, recounting our adventures.

"I had to hitchhike clear to Peoria," my older brother scolded merrily. "*Me*, the leading man . . ." He lifted an elegant two-toned shoe—with a flapping sole—"In these!"

"But by golly, you got here." Dad's chubby face was beaming. Then suddenly he broke down—Dad, who never cried. "We're together!"

Together. The best present we could give one another, we realized. All of us. Just being here in the old house where we'd shared so many Christmases. No gift on our lavish lists, if they could materialize, could equal that. . . .

In most Christmases since that memorable one we've been lucky. During the years our children were growing up there were no separations. Then one year, appallingly, history repeated itself. For valid reasons, not a single faraway child could get home. Worse, my husband had flown to Florida for some vital surgery. A proud, brave man—he was adamant about our not coming with him "just because it's Christmas," when he'd be back in another week.

Like my mother before me, I still had one lone chick left—Melanie, fourteen. "We'll get along fine," she said, trying to cheer me.

We built a big fire every evening, went to church, wrapped presents, pretended. But the ache in our hearts kept swelling. And the day before Christmas we burst into mutual tears. "Mommy, it's just not right for Daddy to be down there alone!"

"I know it." Praying for a miracle, I ran to the telephone. The airlines were hopeless, but there was one roomette available on the last train to Miami. Almost hysterical with relief, we threw things into bags.

And what a Christmas Eve! Excited as conspirators, we cuddled together in that cozy space. Melanie hung a tiny wreath in the window and we settled down to watch the endless pageantry flashing by to the rhythmic clicking song of the rails. . . . Little villages and city streets—all dancing with lights and decorations and sparkling Christmas trees. . . . And cars and snowy countrysides and people—all the people. Each one on his or her special pilgrimage of love and celebration this precious night.

At last we drifted off to sleep. But hours later I awoke to a strange stillness. The train had stopped. And, raising the shade, I peered out on a very small town. Silent, deserted, with only a few lights still burning. And under the bare branches, along a lonely street, a figure was walking. A young man in sailor blues, head bent, hunched under the weight of the sea bag on his shoulders. And I thought—*home! Poor kid, he's almost home.* And I wondered if there was someone still up waiting for him; or if anyone knew he was coming at all. And my heart cried out to him, for he was suddenly my own son—and my own ghost, and the soul of us all—driven, so immutably driven by this annual call, "Come home!"

Home for Christmas. There must be some deep psychological reason why we turn so instinctively toward home at this special time. Perhaps we are acting out the ancient story of a man and a woman and a coming child, plodding along with their donkey toward their destination. It was necessary for Joseph, the earthly father, to go home to be taxed. Each male had to return to the city of his birth.

Birth. The tremendous miracle of birth

shines through every step and syllable of the Bible story. The long, arduous trip across the mountains of Galilee and Judea was also the journey of a *life* toward birth. Mary was already in labor when they arrived in Bethlehem, so near the time of her delivery that in desperation, since the inn was full, her husband settled for a humble stable.

The child who was born on that first Christmas grew up to be a man. Jesus. He healed many people, taught us many important things. But the message that has left the most lasting impression and given the most hope and comfort is this: that we do have a home to go to, and there will be an ultimate home-coming. A place where we will indeed be re-united with those we love.

Anyway, that's my idea of Heaven. A place where Mother is standing in the door, probably bossing Dad the way she used to about the turkey or the tree, and he's enjoying every minute of it. And old friends and neigh-bors are streaming in and out and the sense of love and joy and celebration will go on forever.

A place where every day will be Christ-mas, with everybody there together. At home.

Mothers and Daughters

Oh, God, help all mothers to draw closer to their daughters because of Christmas.

Because Mary was once a daughter in Galilee and had a mother who loved her. A mother who must have worried about her even as we mothers worry today.

It couldn't have been easy for Anna, Lord, discovering her daughter was going to have a child. How many nights did she lie awake? How many hours did she pace the floor? How many agonizing hours did she pray?

And, even after Joseph believed and took Mary home to love and care for, how did Anna feel when they packed up and set off for Bethlehem? Her daughter, little more than a child herself, going away with her new husband to bear her baby so far from home.

Did Anna worry then, too, Lord? Did she walk the floor again, awaiting news? Did she hunger to hold her first grandchild in her arms, during those many long months that must be endured before the little family returned?

Oh, God, because of this very human misery that must have been suffered even through the miracle, help all mothers and daughters to draw closer together today.

Let us talk to each other more. Trust each other more. Love each other more. And, whatever the periods of our separation, actual or otherwise, let us both know that with your help there is always a time of reunion. We can find each other again. We can come home to each other.

Trimming Your Special Tree

The true flavor and spirit of a family is captured and expressed in its Christmas tree.

Even the species is important. If you're used to a certain kind, no other will do. "We always have a long-needled pine," one neighbor says, gesturing to the silvery plumage in the corner. "It just wouldn't seem like Christmas with anything else."

And you nod and smile and lavishly admire the truly beautiful stranger with its trimmings, though privately wondering how anybody could imagine Christmas without the spicy scent of the fir tree you have always been accustomed to.

The size is likewise significant. Short fat

trees, looking as cozy and roly-poly as Santa himself, are the choice of some people. Others want them slender and tall. Still others like them small enough to be set upon a table. "We've always done it that way and we like it better, somehow."

Some people even like artificial trees. "That way we don't have to go traipsing around looking for a fresh one.

"The tree goes into storage with the trimmings and comes out faithfully every year, like an old friend. Ours has been with us such a long time now, I hate to think of ever having to replace it."

The placing of the tree becomes traditional, a part of family character too. A favorite window where its shining lights toss a gay greeting to people passing in the streets. Or a nook in the den—"It's cozy back there; we all go there and build a big fire and sit around on the floor and don't mind the mess." Or sometimes in the recreation room. "It's where we have all our parties; it just seems the logical place for the tree."

Then there is the timing of the raising of this vital visitor. "We put ours up at least a week before Christmas and enjoy it then. But the day after Christmas we take it down and throw it out—I can hardly wait to get rid of the mess." To some this is the only way to do it; to others such haste is sheer heresy. "We always trim our tree on Christmas Eve. It's new and all ready for the big day—just like the children dressed up in their party clothes. And it stays dressed up and beautiful until New Year's."

No matter when you bring your tree home and put it up, there is the rasp of a saw and the good resin smell of wood as your husband kneels on the porch, cutting the trunk and trimming the tip and building a stand to replace the one that you always mean to save each year. . . .

The branches swish and whisper as the tree is ushered into the house. It sways and bows like a great if rather unsteady grand dame as you lean it this way and that and spread its green skirts and arrange its flowing branches. "A little to the right—no, left now, left, that's got it. Oh, it's lovely!"

The trimming also reflects the household's personality. Some people like their trees all silver or gold or white or perhaps all blue. I even saw one tree that was a fabulous pink, adorned in live pink carnations. But such trees are usually confined to the sophisticated or the childless.

To the average American family there is nothing like an old-fashioned green one, smelling as if fresh from the forest, and trimmed with a hodgepodge of icicles and tinsel and ornaments straight from the dime store, along with paper chains and thingamabobs fashioned by little fingers and hung there eagerly.

Children dash to the attic to bring down the old, familiar trimmings: Strings of slightly tarnished tinsel. A one-legged Santa. A bird in a gilded cage. Balls that have mysteriously survived the years. . . . New ones are unwrapped, and grabbed—and some of them broken in a bright tinkling spill. . . . "Now children, wait, don't get so hasty, let Daddy put the lights on first—"

"That reminds me, where's the double socket? Anybody seen a sack of bulbs?"

"Say, let's call up some other kids to help us!" Offspring dash to the phone. . . . "Come over right away quick, we're going to trim the tree!" . . .

Sighing, you and your husband regard each other. "Oh, I guess a few more underfoot won't hurt." Experimentally, he plugs in the lights and the tree is flooded in a cascade of color—amber, blue-green, rose. . . .

You stand for a moment, admiring. "Actually it hardly needs anything else!"

You touch his shoulder lightly, heading for the kitchen to see how the cookies are holding out and wondering if the children will want to string popcorn.

Because no matter what the kind of tree chosen, the place and manner of its shining, or the hour of its debut, it sings a common song—becomes for a season the common symbol of joy and love in the family.

The Christmas Spirit

Oh, Lord, it can't last, I know it can't last—this sense of joy I feel, this mounting sense of love and understanding and delight in all the world.

It is rising in me like a fountain. I want to dance with it, I want to sing, I want to draw all living creatures into its magical circle to share its radiance, to experience its wonder.

This gift of yours, this sweet inexplicable gift of the Christmas spirit. Why is it so long in coming to some of us? And why can't everyone have it always? Why must it be so brief?

Why must it dwindle and vanish when the season of Christmas is past and we have returned

*to the tasks and troubles of every day? Why must
peace and good will be limited to these beautiful
days of celebration?*

*The Christmas spirit is like a baptism, Lord.
It is your holy spirit, surely, baptizing us with the
innocent joy of the newborn king. It makes us
kings, too, for a little while. It makes us feel like
newborn gods.*

*Oh, Lord, thank you for the Christmas spirit.
And "take not thy Holy Spirit from us," in the
days when Christmas is past.*

"Welcome Home!"

They're spilling off from buses, they're
pouring from the trains and planes and cars—
all the children coming home from school or
the service of their country for the holidays.

In houses everywhere telephones jingle.
Or mothers and fathers in markets hail each
other with the eager question: "When's Johnny
getting home? Our Betty's due at midnight
tonight!" A kind of reaching out with a happy
question, in order to hear one's own voice im-
parting your own delicious news: He's coming.

. . . She's coming. . . . Our children will soon be home!

Let's see now, consult your shopping list for the special things they like. Sour cream, dill pickles, ripe olives, chow mein—all those ridiculous whims you used to scold them for, but which now seem such sheer joy to gather in good supply.

What pleasure, too, to tidy up the too-long-silent room. No matter that it will be a cyclone of suitcases tomorrow, and in two days the old exasperating mess of bureau drawers open, books scattered about, and apple cores, and clothes in a heap on the floor.

For the first few moments at least it must be lovely. Tidy, attractive, every dusted shelf, every bright clean curtain at the window radiating the heart behind it that shouts, so joyously, "Welcome, home!"

Silent Night

Now it is Christmas Eve. . . . The things I had worried about didn't happen. The things I had dreaded are all happily achieved. You gave me the strength, you gave me the time, you gave me the means, as you always have!

And now, in this little time when the family are gone on last-minute errands, my heart is full. I stand in joy and gratefulness taking inventory:

The tree stands in the window; its winking lights spill little rainbows on the snowy sill, and bestow a friendly blessing on people passing by.

The turkey is stuffed and waiting. The final cards, incredibly, have all been mailed. The house is fragrant with pies cooling in the kitchen . . . pine boughs on the mantel . . . and the wood smoke of the fire. I draw this warm essence into my being, and am grateful.

I see our gifts, tinseled and tied and full of mystery, beneath this radiant tree. Amused and marveling, I think of all the other packages I fretted and stewed over, safely arrived at their destinations, now reposing like these, full of mystery and promise, beneath other trees.

Now thank you, Lord, for my family and bless their safe return. Bless us as we sing the carols, hear the ancient story. Enter into us as we smell the candles and the incense. So that we know with all our beings that this event was real, and you are real; that we are truly one with you and with the holy family.

Oh, Lord, please bless our family. Our very human, faulty family, as we share this greatest miracle of all—the living gift of love that came that Silent Night.

"I've Got a Date
for Christmas Eve"

Episode on Christmas Eve . . .

"Now Mom, this new girl I'm dating and I have got plans all set for Christmas Eve. So don't object," your son warns.

"My goodness, why should I?" you ask. "You're practically grown."

"That's right. And so is she. Besides, I've worked and earned the money—I can afford to take her to a good nightclub."

"Nightclub?" There's no disguising your distress. "On Christmas Eve?"

"That's right. She's never been to one. I know you'd rather have me stick around trimming the tree and all that jazz, but a bunch of us are going, we've got our plans all made."

Protests, you know would be futile. Besides—you agreed. On the big night he comes down looking both festive and sophisticated. Best dark suit, scarlet vest. But needing help with his tie. "Wait'll you meet her, she's great. I'll bring her by."

The tree-trimming is in full swing when they arrive. The young people all troop in to be admired. Gaily they toss a handful of icicles toward the branches, hang an ornament. The little children, in pajamas, are awed before this worldly visitation—middle ones vaguely wistful—the girls are so gorgeous in their party clothes, the boys so dashing.

You all crowd in the doorway, waving them off. "Good-bye, have a good time." But the fire seems to crackle less brightly now. There is something vaguely lonely about even the splendidly shining tree. You begin to clean up the mess. Order, "Get to bed now, or Santa's liable to drive those reindeer right on past our chimney."

"Yaaah, Santa Claus!"

"Don't talk like that—he'll hear you!"

You get them settled at last, stir up the fire, heat the coffee, and begin the annual discussion about how to manage midnight church services.

"Let's go together," your husband says. "It's so close, and they're old enough to leave."

"I wish we *could* all go together."

"Now if you're worrying about what I think you are, forget it. Kids have to grow up, make their own decisions."

You get dressed. Go to the door to check the weather. It is beginning to snow—like a frail blessing. The flakes are white and soft as a baby's receiving blanket. Church bells ring out on the crisp cold air. "Come, come!" they call.

And as you stand there, a car pulls up to the curb. Figures spill out, come laughing up the walk. "We're back!" they announce.

"What happened?" you exclaim. "Wouldn't they let you *in?*"

"Oh, sure they let us in—and boy did they take our money! When we found out how much it cost, we were almost scared to order."

"And it was so dark," wails one of the girls. "Nobody could see how beautiful we are!"

"Besides"—your son draws you aside, confides half sheepishly—"it just didn't feel right being there. Not on Christmas Eve. We figured if we hurried we could still make the services. C'mon, let's go to church!"

Happy Day

God, bless the chaos of Christmas Day.

Now it's hark, the herald angels, who scurry down the hall at daybreak, pounding on doors, proclaiming, "Merry Christmas, get up!"

Bless the very urgency with which they drag

us downstairs. (Farewell, fleeting glimpse of order and beauty—packages in enticing stacks, toys neatly displayed beneath the shining tree.)

Bless the frantic, joyful wreckage that ensues. Let me be thankful for that too. For this is the end of suspense, the hour of discovery.

Thank you for the wanton welter of papers, ribbons, tags. All this abundance, Lord. All this joyful confusion. Though I am distracted by it, let me rejoice in it. For this is a birthday celebration. And birthday parties weren't meant to be orderly. God, bless the sleigh bells jangling on the door as people come and go.

Thank you for the voices, the laughter, and that people are too filled with loving excitement to stay apart on this climactic day. God, bless the happy confusion of Christmas dinner. The extra faces, some of them otherwise lonely faces, brightening because they are here.

Thank you for the feasting on turkey, dressing, mince pie.

God, bless even the clutter later. And the leftovers, and the lengthy cleaning up. Now give me an extra spurt of energy to bring some order out of this gloriously tumbled house. But if not tonight, well, tomorrow. . . . For now, let us all just continue to enjoy it. This happy festival to celebrate the coming of the Christ Child: Christmas Day!

Sing a Song of
Christmas Carols

Deck the Halls with Boughs of Holly . . . And wash the curtains and polish the silver. And clean out the fireplace and haul in the wood. . . . And try to find the old tree base. And dig out those cartons of decorations to see how many are good for another year.

While Shepherds Watched Their Flocks by Night . . . Sit up late making doll clothes. And finishing a sweater and painting a sled. And helping your husband uncrate a bicycle . . . And then steal around checking on your own flock before collapsing into bed.

Good Christian Men, Rejoice . . . When the last box is finally wrapped and tied and in the mail, and you're at least halfway through addressing the greeting cards.

We Three Kings of Orient Are . . . Bearing gifts we traverse afar: to church and parties and school bazaars. And shut-ins and hospitals and children's homes. And that family whose mother is ill and whose father is out of a job.

O Come, All Ye Faithful . . . Joyful and triumphant that somehow it's all done! The church bells are ringing, it's time to come. . . . Come, children and neighbors and aunts and uncles and cousins—come and behold him, O come let us adore him!

Away in a Manger . . . No crib for a bed— a three-year-old is curled up in a pew, fast asleep.

It Came Upon the Midnight Clear . . . That little voice calling out: "Is it morning yet? Did Santa Claus come?"

Silent Night, Holy Night . . . All is calm, all is bright . . . at last . . . It is, it truly is . . . Sleep in heavenly peace.

Hark! the Herald Angels Sing . . . At the crack of dawn, "Get up, get up. Merry Christmas!"

Joy to the World . . . Let earth receive her king. . . . And people their gifts, and parents their hugs . . . Let children run back and forth to each other's houses, and neighbors pop in for a cup of wassail and to admire the shining tree. . . . Let heaven and nature and your own heart sing!

God Rest You Merry, Gentlemen . . . And women. Let nothing you dismay! Even though the whole house is an explosion of candy, nuts, papers, presents and ribbons; the tags are so mixed up, nobody knows who to thank for what; and the cat is knocking the ornaments off the tree.

Add another log to the fire snapping so

fragrant on the grate, baste the turkey already golden in the oven. Fling open the door to grandparents and other guests who come tramping up the snowy walk. With true love and brotherhood, each other now embrace.

God rest you merry—mothers and fathers and families and friends, at the end of this glorious Christmas Day!

Here Lies

Underneath the mistletoe,
Underneath the tree,
Underneath the tinsel,
The pajamas, the candy,
The turkey, the carolers,
The giggling, the bawling,
The stockings, the eggnog,
The shaving lotion,
The puppy, the toys, the fruitcake . . .
Here lies Me!

—Hope Appelbaum

These Things, Too, Are Christmas

They were playing with their dolls at the foot of the cluttered tree. And as they tugged fat rubber arms into pink sweaters, tied bonnets, or combed out rooted hair, I overheard this bit of philosophizing:

"The thing I like best about Christmas, besides the presents, of course, is how *nice* everybody is to everybody. Wouldn't it be nice if everybody could keep on being nice like that all year?"

"I'll say, like teachers not getting so cross when you can't find your boots and stuff. Why, my teacher was so nice the last day she looked actually pretty for a change!"

"Or your folks not yelling at you so much. And the fun of doing things for people. It's funny—at Christmas you really *want* to!"

"Yeah, like stuffing those stockings for the Salvation Army. Why, I put in this little toy bath set I wouldn't even let my sister *play* with, let alone give away!"

And they sat marveling together over the change that seems to come over all of us at Christmas. And, even as adults, bemoaning the fact that good will is like bright birds which appear for a season and then must go winging away.

But must it? Does it really? Is good will any the less wonderful or heartwarming because it becomes scattered? Because it lights on so many unexpected branches throughout the year?

A child is born—and suddenly all the people in the neighborhood are calling each other in glad excitement, and planning a shower. That too is Christmas. . . .

An election campaign is over, and people who have been arch political rivals stand together watching an Inaugural Parade. "Say, it's cold, wanta share my blanket? Let me hold your little boy for a minute so he can see. Aren't they a handsome family? I didn't vote for him, but now—" That too is Christmas. . . .

A bus driver goes out of his way to help a bewildered foreigner. . . . A headwaiter gives the best table to a family who obviously seldom dine out, and slip the children a treat. . . . Busy women go regularly to places like Junior Village to leave a bit of mothering there. . . .

All these things too are Christmas. We

can see them if we watch, and hear their bright songs if we listen, all through the year.

"Dear Grandma, Thanks for the Wollet"

Memory pictures . . .

The children whom you've browbeaten into writing their thank-you notes sit in the glow of the Christmas tree. Its light pours over their bent heads and there is earnest, troubled concentration on their faces.

"Where's my new stationery that somebody sent me?" A plaid-shirted son scrambles among the pile of presents at his feet.

"Lucky! You got stationery—nobody gave me any; guess I'll have to use notebook paper."

"Now, dear, no," you remonstrate. "Use some of my notepaper—unless Brother will lend you some of his."

"Well—just one piece," he yields grouchily. "This has got to last me—"

"Yeah, to write to all his girls!"

Arguments are eased; pens are found,

pencils, sufficient paper. "What'd Aunt Margaret send me? What'll I say?"

They settle down. There is a hushed, mouselike scratching. It mingles with the hiss and crackle of the fire, the sound of a branch against the window, the tick of rain that may turn to snow. The twinkling colors of the tree and the firelight bathe them in a rosy glow. They yawn and scratch and bend to the task before them: "Dear Grandma—Thank you for the wollet that you sent me, I like it very very—*How do you spell much?*" . . . "Dear Cousin Pam—"

You stand at the window, pull back the curtain. The air is filled with a misty shining, the streets are black satin, car lights go boring down golden tunnels. . . . If the rain turns to snow before morning, perhaps they can use their sleds. . . .

The Christmases Children Remember

One year, when grown sons and daughters came home for Christmas, we had fun showing old movies of Christmases past. Laughing and pointing, we relived the merry commotion: hanging up stockings, trimming the tree, the year the cat got tangled up in tinsel and the lights went out. Shots of the church pageant Christmas Eve—two little shepherd boys in bathrobes, one solemn, one waving to Mommy as they marched onstage. Prized glimpses of their sister dancing in the *Nutcracker Suite.* Even some of the whole family on the Washington mall at the national Pageant of Peace. But mostly scenes of excited children rushing downstairs Christmas morning to claim the dazzling plunder under the tree.

Then as we put away the films, I was surprised to hear them discussing other Christmases they remembered even more vividly. "The year we adopted that family—what was their name?" Mark asked. "Dad heard about them at the office, and we all got busy buying or making stuff. Toys for the kids, and I think we even found something for the parents. Anyway, Dad let me help pick out the turkey, and a couple of us went along to deliver it."

"He made us stay in the car when we got there, though," his brother spoke up. "Afraid it might embarrass them—just carried it to the back door where their father was waiting. I think the poor guy was crippled—anyway I'll never forget how he straightened up and waved to us. Or those little faces peeking out the window."

"That wasn't the only family we helped," his sister Mickie reminded us. "Why, we did that for several years." And they began to compare experiences of things I'd almost forgotten.

"What I remember most is the time we made all those stuffed animals and Raggedy Anns for the Doll House downtown to give away. I helped Mother sew them up; you younger kids did the stuffing, and she took you along on the streetcar to deliver them. I can still see you lugging those shopping bags. Boy, were you excited!"

"I cried," Melanie confessed dramatically. "I was selfish, I wanted to *keep* my Raggedy Andy. But when I handed him over, I was so thrilled I almost exploded!"

On and on they went. Not once mentioning anything they *got*—even a first bicycle, a special doll, a single gift desperately wanted. Instead, all the memories that seemed significant were experiences in *giving:* The time we invited the whole Brownie troop to the house to fill stockings for the Salvation Army. The Scouts who mended broken sleds and trains for others in our basement. The years when our daughters were old enough to work beside me at the Salvation Army Toy Center. Donning their bright red aprons with us, they led needy parents through the entrancing display, helping them pick out gifts for their children.

"Those little red aprons," Melanie laughed. "Oh, Mother, I hope I have daughters myself someday so we can do things like that together. That was the best part of Christmas."

"It sure was," the others agreed. "It gave all of us memories we'll never forget." They expressed only one regret: How nice it would be now to see movies or even snapshots of some of these things too. "If only we had *those* pictures!"

Then both Mark and Mallory spoke up. "Sure, but we don't need them. We were all doing something more important. That's why we remember. People don't need pictures to remember things that really matter."

Listening, I realized my sons were right. The memories they cherished most were beyond the scope of films and movie cameras; they could be engraved only on their hearts.

Chapter 8

THE CHRISTMAS
LOVE STORY

The Good Stepfather

I have always had a special fondness
for Joseph. A special curiosity about
him, a special sympathy. I think of him not
only at Christmas, but often when I see good
fathers. And particularly good stepfathers.

What a wonderful man Joseph must have
been. It couldn't have been easy for him, learning that the woman he was engaged to, plan-

ning to marry, was going to have a child. A child that was not his child! What a blow to his manhood, to his credulity, and if he loved her (as I think he did) to his heart.

The Bible doesn't tell us much about Joseph, but there is one significant phrase: "Being a just man, and not willing to make her a public example, he was minded to put her away quietly—" What soul-searching he must have suffered before this decision, what anguish before the angel's revelation. "Being a just man," he would not think of hurting her. And perhaps this decision to "put her away," even quietly, was because he deemed it might be best for *her*. For Mary and the holy child she was to bear—since he could offer so little as a carpenter in Nazareth.

It couldn't have been easy for him either, leading the donkey with its precious burden so many miles to Bethlehem. And yet how strong and kind and dependable he was. Finding them room in the stable (which was actually a cave), watching over them. Carrying them safely into Egypt, protecting and supporting them until they dared return. Then teaching his own trade to this son—the son of God who became, through love, his son.

What a fine stepfather Joseph was, doing

all that a natural father would have done. Perhaps even more in some ways. He seems to me a perfect example of all good husbands who stand by the women they love, to protect and cherish them. Of all men who strive to be the best possible fathers to their children—even when those children may not be their own flesh and blood.

The Christmas Eve
I Smelled the Hay

Christmas Eve and we were late, as usual, herding our family into the hushed candlelit church. The last bell had stopped ringing; every seat was taken. The usher had to lead us up a side aisle to some steps, where we could perch behind the choir loft, so close to the manger scene we could smell the hay.

Real hay . . . its pungent scent transporting me back to the sweet-smelling hayfields of my childhood. The barns, the mangers. Suddenly I was shaken by a vivid sense of reality. For the first time in my life I realized, "Why, this *really happened!* There actually *was* a girl who had a baby far from home—in a manger, on the hay." A very young girl, probably—because I had recently heard or read that in the culture of Mary's time a girl was betrothed as soon as she went into her womanhood, and married before the year was out.

My own daughter Melanie, thirteen, who had just matured, was sitting beside me. And I thought, astonished, "Why, Mary couldn't have been much older than Melanie—perhaps fourteen—when she bore the Christ Child!"

With this awareness came a thrilling conviction about Joseph. He must have been a young man too; old enough to protect and care for her and the child, but young enough to be deeply in love with Mary. And she with him! Why not? They were betrothed to be married. Surely God, who loved us enough to send his precious son into the world, would want that child to be raised in a home of love. A place where there was genuine human love between the two who were chosen to be his earthly parents.

I left the church in a state of great excitement. I knew I must write their story. I must make this blessed event as real for other people as it had become for me. That's when I thought of writing *Two From Galilee*. That wonderful Christmas Eve when I smelled the hay.

The Nativity from
Two From Galilee

As Mary's hour drew nearer, she found herself wanting her mother. More and more often she climbed the hillside to be with Hannah for a while. "So you've come," Hannah would say flatly, belying the pleasure in her eyes. "Here, knead the dough and set it near the oven to rise." It was good to be near Hannah in the old way, being ordered about. It was curiously like being a little girl again.

One day when they were at the dyeing in the yard she asked, "When my time comes, you will serve me as midwife, won't you, Mother?"

Hannah turned from the steaming kettle. "But if this is God's doing, if indeed it is the miracle you believe, why then will you have need of a crude servant like me?"

"I don't know. There is still so much that I don't understand. As you say, another miracle may happen to bring this divine child forth from me. Yet I must be prepared, since I don't know." There was a look of patient bewilderment on Mary's face. "It's the not knowing that's hard. It's that, only that, of which I confess I'm afraid."

The air between them was heightened and sweetened by this coming event that now concerned them both. Thus when Joseph came up one Sabbath eve to join Mary and her parents for the evening meal, they were astounded at his news.

Word of a decree from Caesar had reached Nazareth only a few hours before. "New taxes are going to be levied throughout the entire Roman world," Joseph told them in quiet outrage. "And to make sure nobody fails to pay, they're going to take a new census. They've ordered every adult male citizen to proceed at once to the place of his birth to be registered and counted. For me, that means traveling to Bethlehem."

"But you can't go." Hannah voiced their astonished protest. "You can't leave Mary."

"He has no choice." Joachim moved to the corner where the sacred scrolls and instruments of ceremony were kept. The house was fragrant with the foods that the women had been preparing all day; it was to have been a happy evening. "None of us has." Joachim was scowling, his voice fierce. "To defy those accursed swine would mean being thrown into prison. As if our taxes weren't enough to break our backs, now they must count us like beasts of the fields."

As he spoke, two final blasts from the trumpets came thrilling through the night, signaling the time for the women to light their Sabbath lamps. The sweet-smelling wine was poured, and they strove to be at peace, reciting together the sacred words of the prayers. But anxiety was upon them, and afterward, instead of discussing the Scriptures or singing psalms, they could speak of nothing but this latest insult, with its terrible complications.

"I'll have to prepare for the trip as soon as the Sabbath is over," Joseph told Joachim. "I should leave early in the week. Fortunately my brothers can register here and look after the shop." He gazed sadly at Mary, who was helping Hannah clear the table, the only work they might do and not break the rules of rest. "As for Mary, my mother will look after her while I'm gone."

Hannah turned swiftly from the cupboard. "We'll look after her," she said, and for a moment she could not conceal her exultation. To have him out of the way at such a time! To bring the child into the world with her own hands, be the first to know it, love it; and for Joachim to be the first male to consecrate it by holding it upon his knees.

But Mary had shaken the last crumbs from

the cloth and crossed the room to stand by Joseph's side. "I want to go with you," she said.

"Mary, you can't. My beloved, you can't."

"He's right," Hannah said fiercely. "It's unthinkable. The mountains are treacherous in the winter, and the nights are freezing. You might lose the child."

"I cannot lose the child."

"And what if your time comes upon you somewhere out in the wilderness among the jackals?" Hannah was in a frenzy.

"We will take shelter," Mary said. "We will be safe."

"Mary . . ." Joseph gripped her hands. "Mary, you had better listen to your mother."

"Joachim, speak to her," Hannah beseeched her husband.

Joachim ran a big trembling hand across his grizzled jaw. Slowly he shook his head. "She must do what she must do."

"I must go with my husband," said Mary. "I must journey with him to Bethlehem."

For four days they traveled, south through the old towns of Nain, Sunem and Jezreel, then eastward until they reached the

Jordan; then southward through its valley until they must climb again into the bleak hills of Judea.

Joseph had fashioned a saddle to fit on the donkey's back, and Mary rode along beside her husband, uncomplaining either of the cold or the fierce contrast of the wind, blowing its hot, stifling breath from the desert. Despite the dirt, the jolting, all the discomfort, Mary smiled a great deal, half in her pleasure at simply being with Joseph, half in a reverie of the coming child. She smiled faintly even as she dozed— as she was dozing now, on this day that Joseph hoped would be nearly the last one of their journey.

His feet were sore, his whole body un-utterably weary, but he knew he could not be half so miserable as she. He halted the donkey and stood for a moment gazing upon her where she sat, her head forward on her chest. He stood there wondering if there was anything he could do to make her more comfortable. The marvel of her electing to come with him seemed more than he deserved. "Mary, have you any idea how beautiful you are?"

She laughed. "Oh, Joseph, dirty and di-sheveled as I am?"

He laid his cheek against hers. Then he took a handkerchief from his girdle and, pour-

ing a little water from one of the bags, proceeded to wash her dusty face, if only to cool
it a little. "Would you like me to lift you down
so that you can stretch?"

"Yes, I need to walk about a bit." He set
her down, and she stood there trying to take
in her surroundings. "I must have slept. Where
are we?"

"There's the river. By nightfall we should
be in Jericho. And tomorrow night, if all goes
well, we shall sleep in Bethlehem."

"I hope so." She had not realized how
weak and trembling her legs were until she
was standing. Her body ached, her back was
one fierce cramp, and the child was thrashing
about so that it was hard to speak. She drew
a deep breath, still smiling determinedly. "The
sooner we can reach Bethlehem, the better it
will be."

"Are you all right, my beloved?" he asked
anxiously.

"Yes. Yes—it's only riding so long.
Come, I'll walk beside you."

"Very well then, I'll ride." Joseph
laughed.

"Would that you could. Poor Joseph.
Would that you had a camel to ride, or a horse
like the Romans."

"Would that you were right, for then I

would be rich and able to provide so much better for you and your child," he said.

"Our child," she said. "This child that the Lord has vouchsafed into our keeping. Oh, Joseph, just because it is my body that will bear him does not mean that he is any less your child than mine."

"I didn't father him," he said quietly. "Even you must agree that there's no way to change that fact."

"No." She pressed his hand, trying to think how to comfort him. "And yet—" She groped for the words to express it. "In many ways he will be more your son than mine."

"More!"

"Yes, more," she insisted. "A father is so important in Israel. A son needs his father to teach him the ways of the world, and of God and the Law. Once I have borne and suckled this child, my task will be largely finished. But yours will be only beginning."

"He may not need a father's training. He who will come to us as the very Son of God."

"Perhaps he will need it more. I—I don't know much about it, but I feel in my heart that he will come to us innocent and uninformed, a child like any child, needing guidance from us as well as from the One who sends him.

Both of us, Joseph, but you especially. And that's why you were chosen. For you *were* chosen—your honor is as great as mine."

She spoke with such conviction that a thrill of hope ran through him. He knew that she was seeing this only as she wished to, because she loved him. He knew that he would never be as significant as Mary in the eyes of God, nor would he have it so. But her words had given him new purpose.

That evening as Joseph was making camp he snared a partridge, which he blessed and then bled and roasted over the coals. Mary had already started the quick bread that she baked for them each night. It always tasted of smoke, but it was delicious after the cold dry bread and figs they had eaten at noon. Tonight they were ravenous, and the unusual treat of the meat made the meal festive. They sat beside their fire, eating and watching the stars come out.

"Our last night on the road," Mary said wistfully. "For some reason I almost hate to have this journey end."

"Yes, it's been good, just the two of us like this." Now that it was nearly over, Joseph too had a strange wish to prolong it. Something was ending here, this night. A phase of their life was ending.

He fed the fire another load so that it crackled and sprang high, and then he put down a pallet of cloaks and skins for Mary and rolled her up in them. They had never been happier, nor the heavens more beautiful. The sky was almost too crowded with stars: now and then one darted off in bright escape. The constellations drew their jeweled patterns, crisp and clear. They could hear some shepherds singing on a nearby hillside and see the eye of their campfire glowing like a hearth. The voices drifted down to them, and the occasional plaintive crying of the sheep. It was companionable having them so close: it was like having neighbors by their star-canopied home.

Sunrise found them again on their way. They tried in vain to recapture last night's mood, but a sense of urgency was upon them. They were nervous before the impending events: the taxes, the census, the birth. And now there was a new worry: Where would they go if there was no room at the inn? For suddenly from side roads and hillsides other people had come streaming in. The press was so great it was scarcely possible to see the

Temple in the distance, when at last they reached the outskirts of the Holy City. But by then Mary was too miserable to care.

"Hurry! Oh, Joseph, hurry," she begged. Every instinct warned her that her time was not far off, and it must not happen before they reached Bethlehem, as foretold by the prophets. Therefore, she reasoned, it could not happen elsewhere. Yet anxiety warred with that blind conviction.

Joseph pleaded with those in his path, trying to maneuver around them with the heavily laden donkey. It was a little better once they were beyond Jerusalem. It was much cooler here, but the donkey was cruelly burdened. He could move only so fast, especially since the road now climbed again into the barren hills. This day the sun shone pale and chilly. Gusts of stinging grit tormented the cheeks and eyes. The road was clotted with people and their mounts, litters, or carts, all of them weary, impatient. The smell of garlic and oil and sweat and dusty clothes together with that of beasts was almost overpowering. Mary had to fight nausea now, along with the grinding anguish that began to gnaw slowly at her back, then in waves at her very vitals, so that she would have doubled over if she could, clutching herself and moaning. But she must sit erect, hanging on. . . .

They were not too far now from the Bethlehem gates, where a mass of humanity surged, anxious to have their goods weighed and be done with the tax collectors stationed there so that they could enter the town. A couple of Roman centurions on magnificent horses rode about, trying to keep order. "Don't crowd, get in line now, get your belongings ready. The tax collectors will take you each in turn."

The donkey had halted. Mary sat dazed, limp from her last bout with the agony, trying to rest. She was dimly aware that Joseph had left her side. She could see that he was saying something to the centurion, and this astounded her, and yet it did not, either. Nothing mattered, nothing except that she hang on to herself until they managed, heaven knew when, to get through the gates and into the inn. The inn, the inn, the bed at the inn . . . dear God, please let there be a bed at the inn.

She saw the centurion suddenly wheel his horse about and wave his whip above the crowd. "Stand back, out of the way, let these people through! You fools, where are your manners?" Many fell back, surprised, as he pulled up beside her. "Are you all right, lady?" he asked, taking off his helmet and mopping his brow where the iron weight had left a deep-red mark. He was very young; his anxious blue eyes did not match his harsh voice.

"Yes," she gasped. "Yes, thank you. Once we get inside . . . into the inn . . ."

But when he had broken a path for them and led them forward and ridden on, the crowd closed in upon them. They resented his having put these Galilean bumpkins at the head of the line. Joseph stood scarlet but adamant, trying to protect their place. And Mary suffered afresh for what he was enduring on her account. Oh, help us, help the tax collectors to hurry!

But the process of weighing, measuring, and assessing proceeded slowly. The collectors at the gate got a percentage, and they made sure that nothing, no garment, no trinket, no grain of meal was held back. It was an eternity before the party ahead of them was finally motioned on and Joseph was called. "Next! Unload and be quick about it."

Joseph had already unstrapped the pannier and lifted down the bundles. All must be exposed, all their poor little possessions. Even—and this was most outrageous and hurtful of all—the lovingly wrapped packet of swaddling clothes. "Is that all?" The tax collector exchanged an amused glance with the other collector as he fingered their goods and slapped them onto the scales.

"Yes," said Joseph tightly.

"What about that thing your wife's sitting on? I presume it's your wife?" he joked, while the crowd tittered.

"Just an old robe that serves to keep her warm at night," Joseph said, again tightly.

"Let's have it."

"Please." Joseph's contempt surpassed that of his tormentor. "Can't you see that my wife is in no condition to climb down? If there is a grain of decency in you, don't disturb her."

"Let it be, then." The man brazened it out. "We'll take your word—one drachma for the old robe. That'll be five dinars altogether. Pay up, pack up and move on."

With unsteady hands, Joseph brought forth the coins. Five dinars! Out of the twelve they had brought for the trip. It was robbery. He flung the money onto the table and savagely stuffed the things back into the bags. But at least they had cleared the gates and could find a place for Mary. He forced a smile as he strapped the panniers back on. "It won't be long, my dearest. Be brave, I'll soon have a place where you can rest."

She nodded, too grateful to speak.

The donkey moved forward, through the gates, into the hubbub of humanity just beyond. The inn stood to the left, a sprawling moss-grown structure with a large courtyard in front and a row of blackened ovens in the rear. The yard was crowded with people unloading baggage, tethering their beasts or leading them through the low doorway that led to the stable beneath the inn. Joseph saw at once that the fears of these last torturous miles were to be realized. Trying to hide his consternation from Mary, he tied the donkey and hastened inside.

The innkeeper was busy serving wine, a squat, wheezing man who had no time for Joseph's appeal. "I'm sorry, we're full up, haven't an inch to lay a cat in—nay, or a mouse. You'll have to do as the others; find yourself a friendly yard to sleep in."

"We can't." Joseph grabbed the man's beefy arm, causing him to slop wine down his grimy apron. "My wife is in labor. She is about to bear a child. You must give us shelter, at least for a few hours."

"But I can't," the innkeeper wheezed. He gestured to the people pounding their mugs for service. "Can't you see for yourself?

There's simply no room. I'm sorry, lad, but I can't perform miracles."

Miracles, Joseph thought in a flash of bitterness. Let the Lord produce one now. "You must," he repeated. "You must help us."

"Well, there is the stable. It's full of creatures and people already, this one below us, but if you don't mind the stink and the noise . . ."

Joseph's heart sank. The chaos was deafening, not only all around them but from below, where he could hear beasts stamping and voices raised in drunken laughter. "Is there nothing else?" he begged.

The innkeeper was gone. But as Joseph plunged back to the entrance, despairing, the man was suddenly wheezing at his side. "Wait. There are some caves toward the back where we store things and stable a few animals when we're crowded. It's quieter there and it's warm; you'd be alone. Just circle around the inn and go down the path; you can't miss it."

Joseph thanked him. But he was heartsick as he hurried back to tell Mary. A stable! That God had chosen him to look after her, and the best he could provide was a poor cave.

But she was in the grip of such pain there was no use wasting time apologizing. "Come," he said gently. "The inn is full, but you'll be alone, my beloved. I'll make you a soft bed on the hay." Taking the donkey by the halter, he hurried it forward.

The pathway pitched downward and led to the opening that marked the first of a series of caves. As he approached through the gathering darkness, he could see that even here they were not to have complete privacy, for a group of grizzled Bedouins had built a fire and were cooking their evening meal. They were laughing and talking and paid scant attention to the little group that plodded into the cave's yawning mouth.

Inside there was the mealy smell of oats and the tang of the animals tethered in the semidarkness. At the far end, groping about, Joseph found what he sensed to be a vacant stall. Hands shaking, he got his lantern lighted and held it high. The place was indeed vacant, with one long manger, a number of tools strewn about, and much clean straw. A kind of storage room. But the straw in the manger was old and rancid. Hanging the lamp in a niche, Joseph cleaned the manger out and pitched the straw aside. Then, working swiftly, he gathered up armloads of the clean dry straw and spread it in the manger. To save time, he flung his own cloak on it.

Then, turning to Mary, he held out his

arms. "I'm sorry, my dearest," he muttered as she slid down. "It's the best I can do."

"Thank God," she moaned softly. "Oh, Joseph, thank God for it and for you." She leaned against him, her forehead cold with sweat. Then she moved toward the place where at last she could lie down. "You must go and fetch a midwife," she panted. "It may be hours before the baby comes, but I must have a woman by my side."

"Yes. I should have thought of that before. I should have inquired at the inn." Again the shock of his appalling ineptitude. Fool, fool. Now he would have to leave her alone and go plunging back into the night.

"Don't worry, I'll be all right." She touched his stricken face. "The pain has stopped altogether," she said, surprised. "Perhaps I can sleep a little."

"I'll not be long, I promise. I'll find someone."

Leaving the lantern behind, he set forth, feeling his way frantically along the stalls. Idiot, blunderer! A stable, among oxen and asses, and not even a woman with her.

"Joseph!" He halted, frozen. It was a

scream too horrifying to believe. He whirled and ran back.

She was sitting upright, her legs dangling over the stall, the tears streaming down her face. "Joseph, don't go, don't leave me! Joseph, it's unbearable, I can't stand it."

"Mary, Mary." He cradled her in his arms, rocking her until the hideous convulsion ceased. Oh, God, he thought. You God. *You* God—if you are a god who performed this miracle—why are you doing this to my beloved?

"I'm sorry," she whispered at length. "Only I got so frightened when it began again and I was alone." She pushed back her tangled hair. "What will we do?" she cried. "You know the ancient taboo—it is not fitting for a man to gaze upon a woman in childbirth."

"And even if it were not so, I know nothing of what to do to help you."

"Go and fetch some water," she said. "Some hot water if you can get it. Go to those herdsmen at the door and see if they can give us some. But don't be long," she begged. "Go no farther even to fetch a midwife."

"I'll send one of them," he said. But even as he ran he heard her moaning.

The herdsmen, who were strumming their

lutes or sprawled about drinking wine, reared up as he burst into the circle of light. "Have you any hot water left from your meal? In heaven's name, help us. My wife is far gone in childbirth, and she needs water and a midwife."

"My friend, the water we can share with you," one of them said, "but there are no midwives among us." There was laughter, but it stopped as they saw Joseph's face. A man rose, tall and dignified in his striped robes, and lifted a steaming pot from the coals. "There is also some barley soup. It is nourishing and still hot. Perhaps that will be of some comfort to your wife. Here, I'll carry it for you and light your way. Meanwhile—" he kicked one of the slumbering boys. "You, Joab, rise up and go into Bethlehem and see if you can find a midwife."

The youth rose, yawning and surly. It was plain he had drunk too much and considered this a joke. But there was no time for Joseph to argue; he must get back to Mary. Carrying the water and followed by the tall shepherd with the soup, Joseph led the way.

The smothered cries from within the little cubicle halted both of them. "Thank you, my friend," Joseph said grimly, and motioned him aside. "If we need anything further, we'll call you." He stole back in and stood where Mary lay, writhing.

"Joseph—oh—Joseph." It came from between her clenched teeth. He could barely hear her, and he fell to his knees beside her, let her grip his hands and pull with all her strength. In their mutual agony it seemed to him that something was being uprooted within him. Self. The last vestige of self. Was this, then, the meaning of love?

"Yes, my dearest, my best beloved?"

"If I die in this, if it destroys me utterly, you must know one thing. I did not sin. You are the only man I have ever loved."

"Hush, my blessed, hush." That this could be uppermost in her mind at such a time seemed to him unutterably pathetic. And that he could have doubted, unendurable. "I know how pure you are. God forgive me for doubting even a minute."

She relaxed a little against his shoulder. Easing her back upon the crackling bed, Joseph rose and swiftly began unloading the donkey. He would need a basin, bowls, linens, so many things. The midwife must come! But whether she did or not, he must be ready.

Pouring a little of the hot water into a basin, he washed his hands. Then he took a dipper of the soup to Mary, and lifting her carefully once again, persuaded her to sip a little. She drank the entire ladle and bade him have some too. Then she lay back. "The midwife—have you sent for her?"

He nodded. "Surely she will be here soon."

"Yes, surely." She was speaking half to reassure herself, half to keep him from worrying. "I wish it could be my mother," she said wistfully.

"Would to God that your mother could be with you." The heat of his words caused her to lift her head. They regarded each other, facing the truth. "Or some woman. I can't leave you, Mary. And if the midwife doesn't come— I'm but a man, without knowledge of these things."

"Don't be afraid." She gripped his hand. "We're forgetting something. That this is God's child, and God will not abandon us."

God's child. She was right. Ignorant and inexperienced though they were, God would let nothing happen to his own child, nor to her who delivered it.

"I must think," Mary said. "While I am still clearheaded, I must instruct you. You must build a fire and keep the swaddling clothes warm. And the water hot. There must be warm water for bathing the baby. And a knife—you must dip it in very hot water before cutting the cord. I have learned that it drives away evil spirits that might harm the child."

"A knife?" Joseph gasped.

"Yes, it must be done. You must do all this if the midwife isn't here."

Joseph's head was beginning to whirl. All these things, these human, physical things—would it come to that, actually? Despite her swollen body and now the pangs of labor, it seemed to him that this which had begun as a miracle would conclude as a miracle. Not so much to spare them, but simply because God's son must come forth in a manner more fitting than to be hurled from a woman's bloody flanks.

He gazed at their lowly surroundings—the oxen and sheep, the little donkey braying piteously for its food, the smell of dung and hay, the cold rock walls glinting in the light of the fire that finally, in desperation, he had been able to coax in the pit he had dug. God's own angels would surely fill the place at the last and lift up Mary and draw from her loins the blessed being without blood or further agony.

The dung and straw and such sticks as he could scrape together began to blaze, lighting up the chamber. And through the chink in the wall he could see one brilliant star, fixed and new, as if the Lord himself had set it there to watch over them. The smoke obscured it, but when the wind shifted, there it was, sparkling.

The pain was the only reality. The pain had become her master, forcing the outcries from her. Yet she must remember that this was no demon that was the author of her torment but the bloody grip of God.

She thought of the beasts being led to be slaughtered at the cold marble tables of the Temple. They were moaning now, moving closer in their condemned files, moaning plaintively—or was it only the low mooing of the cattle in the next stall?

"Joseph, forgive me!" For it was not the cattle she heard but the brute moans and bellowings that came from her own cracked and bitten lips.

"It's all right. Cry if it helps."

The hooves of the poor doomed cattle drove on, over her, crushing her in their path, yet she sought to reassure them: Never fear, sweet cattle, I will bring forth a new kind of offering to Jehovah so that one day you will go bawling to the knife no more. . . . And she sought to reassure the child: Never fear, sweet child, let me not frighten you with my screams. Do not be afraid. Come forth, come forth in triumph out of suffering.

Suffering! A tremendous excitement filled her along with the agony. There was some secret here. If she were not so weary she would understand it—the secret of suffering. Truly to know the Lord God, you must go down into the pit with him, be burned at his fires.

The fires licked at her savagely. God help me, spare me! But she must go with the cattle. They had come charging back for her and were goading her to greater effort with their fierce horns. They were dragging her to the altar with them now, and the god of her pain was driving them all ferociously on. The high priest—it was Joseph who bent near in love and reverence, telling her, "I can see its little head. You must strive harder, beloved."

She obeyed, gratefully. There was a great ripping and flooding and burning, and he came forth out of her, out of Mary, his mother. Thus in blood and pain he came into the world, this son of God who was also man and the son of man.

And Joseph lifted him up for her to see.

And they looked upon him together and marveled at him. His wholeness, infinitely small and red and perfectly formed. And when he squirmed in Joseph's arms and uttered his first cry, the thrill of all mankind ran through both of them, for this was life, human life, and they knew that a miracle had been achieved.

Mary lay drowsing, with the child in her arms, while Joseph busied himself tidying up this small nest that had become for a space their home. How beautiful it was. New strength began to flow through him and, with it, an exaltation. He need berate himself no longer. He had not failed her. Her son had been safely born, and he had helped to bring him forth; that made him in a new and wondrous sense *his* son too. They were sleeping there quietly now, his wife and child. His little family. And, unable to restrain himself, he shielded the lamp and held it above their faces, if only to witness the blessed sight of it in this moment of his rapture.

And as he stood thus he was startled to hear a low rumble of voices, the sound of approaching feet. Fear gripped him, a passion of protectiveness. Like a lion before its den, he went to bar the door. He could see figures carrying torches, though behind them, through the mouth of the cave, such light streamed that it seemed the sun was already high in the skies.

To his relief he saw that the man who led the group was the one who had earlier given him aid. "Hush," Joseph whispered. "Don't wake them. My wife and newborn son are sleeping."

"Then all is well with you, my friend?" the herdsman asked softly. His long, narrow face seemed pale in the glow of the light, his eyes were filled with doubt and amazement. "The child has been safely born?"

"Yes, thanks be to God."

"Then it's true!" There was a smothered outcry, a stir of excitement; the others pressed forward. Among them were several shepherds who had not been with the group in the yard. "We told you this is the place!" one of them said to the Bedouin. "The star led us to it. We have followed it all night, to this very stable, and it stands even now above the door." He begged Joseph, "If you are the father, pray let us come in if only for a minute, that we may see with our own eyes the glory that the angels told us would be waiting in this holy place."

"Angels?"

"A whole chorus of angels," the man said breathlessly. "As we were tending our sheep on the Jericho hills. Please let us come in, if only long enough to deliver the gifts we have brought."

"Joseph?" Mary had roused and was blinking in the strange light that seemed to have claimed the night. "What is it?"

"These men," he told her, shaken. "They are shepherds. They claim to have been guided to this place by a mysterious star. They—they wish to see the little one."

"Then bid them come in." She sat up, there on the hay. Startled, half frightened but smiling, she covered her breast and lifted up the holy child. And the shepherds stole in fearfully, humbly, and laid their gifts at the foot of the manger, rude gifts hastily assembled— some rabbit skins, a sack of figs, a kid, a newborn lamb. And with shining, transfixed faces, they gazed upon the sleeping child, or fell down upon the straw and worshiped him.

For forty days the stable was their home, and each night the great star stood over its entrance. Joseph had never seen such a star, flaming now purple, now white, now gold, its light illuminating the countryside. Dazed, he told Mary, "I'm afraid there will be others coming to see the child."

"Let them come," she murmured. "Oh, Joseph, isn't he lovely? Just look at him—see, his eyes are open, he knows us! He's trying to smile."

"Foolish—all babies smile like that; they don't know what they're doing."

"Oh, but this one does. Our baby does."

Their baby . . . Joseph bent over her where she stood unwinding the swaddling bands. She poured a little oil into her hands and massaged the tiny, squirming body, the flailing fists, the curved, kicking legs. The scent of the baby, ineffably new and tender, stirred Joseph deeply. He bent nearer and offered one of his fingers, and the child clung to it in a thrilling intensity of trust.

Joseph laughed over the pain of his blind adoration. His child. If not the child of his loins, yet still the child of his love. He thought of the ancient taboo, that no man should witness a woman giving birth. Yet God had surely led them to this place where no other woman was. The star outside confirmed it. Had that, too, been a part of God's plan—to include him thus?

Joseph stood one night at the stable door. He had been to the well for water, but he could not go in just yet. The night was cold and clear; it was exhilarating and yet peaceful to stand for a moment before joining his loved ones inside.

Tomorrow they must take the little Jesus and travel to the Temple, there to redeem him with an offering. After that, Joseph reasoned, it would be well to come back to Bethlehem and find work here until the baby was old enough to attempt the treacherous journey back to Nazareth. Would the star follow them? he wondered. Would it continue to blaze above their heads like a torch to light the way?

Where now, star? he thought. Guide me, lead me.

Taking up the cool, bulging skins, he was about to go in when he heard the plunk of approaching hooves and saw, flowing slowly down the pathway from the inn, three camels. He paused, curiously repelled and attracted by the serpentine necks and undulant heads festooned with tassels, the arrogant grace of them as they moved, and the commanding elegance of their riders. Rich merchants, evidently, dark princes from some far country. And it flashed through his consciousness that it was strange they had not summoned a servant to stable their mounts instead of riding down from the inn themselves.

Joseph turned hastily, not wishing to be seen, and was about to dart into the cave when one of them called out to him. "Wait! You there!" The camel drew nearer. "Tell me, is this the place where the new child lies?"

Joseph stood rigid, silent in the grip of a new, terrible apprehension.

"Of course it is, it has to be." The second rider was making a gesture of triumph toward the star. "See, it no longer moves."

"But a stable!" The third rider drew abreast. "Surely this is no fit birthplace for a king."

Joseph's heart had begun to beat in heavy strokes. Obviously these were men of travel and learning, men on a vital mission, and he was afraid. A great foreboding rose up in him. What did such men want with his child? Were the dread, momentous things hinted at so darkly in the prophets already about to begin? He would not have it. Not yet, not yet! The child was not ready; his little life had only just begun.

He stood blocking the entrance as the

strangers prepared to dismount, rapping the beasts on the neck so that they folded their thin legs to crouch.

"Why do you ask?" Joseph demanded. "What do you want?"

"Is there not a newborn child within?"

Joseph hesitated. "Only my wife and son."

They regarded him. One was tall and dark, with a curling black beard. The other two were fairer. All had the look of wisdom and splendor about them, humbling Joseph.

"You are the father then of this holy child?"

"I am the father of a month-old son. And is not every child sacred in the sight of God?"

"Yes. Yes, truly," said the tall one after a second. "But the stars have foretold this event for years. We have studied the stars. We are Magi from Persia and Chaldea, philosophers and physicians, and we have traveled for weeks, following the star that stands over this doorway. It has become the sole purpose of our existence, my friend, to see him, if only for a few minutes, this child of yours who is to change the course of all history. This one who is to become King of the Jews." The voice was grave, at once stern and imploring. "Surely you would not turn us away?"

Joseph gazed into the stranger's impassioned eyes. And he knew that it was ended, the peaceful dream of the stable with only a child at its center and heart. For cradled there in the clay manger lay all the portent and the promise, the man of destiny.

"Wait," he said brusquely. "I must go and consult my wife."

Mary had been packing for the trip. The remains of their evening meal still lay on the table while she attended the baby. He was laughing and crowing as she bent over him to change his swaddling bands. He seemed to recognize Joseph when he entered, to gurgle and glow with new delight. A sweet, desperate pain drove through Joseph's breast. "I'm sorry I was gone so long," he said, "but there are strangers at the door insisting they must see him. They are Wise Men, Mary, come all the way from Persia and Chaldea, they claim."

Mary gasped. "Wise Men? Then you must not keep them waiting." She looked about at the confusion. "Though what will they think of us?"

"Mary, it is the baby they are pressing to see." He caught her hand, and they regarded each other a long moment. "He who is one day to be King of the Jews."

Mary closed her eyes. She too had almost

forgotten, or had set the truth aside. Now she
was forced to remember all the suffering and
hope that had led to this moment. And all the
threat and promise that lay ahead of him—this
innocent little being, kicking and chewing his
fist, unaware of his fate. She took him up and
kissed him; blindly then she put him down and
began preparing the boy so that he should not
be found wanting in the strangers' eyes.

"Bid them come in."

In a few moments she could hear the
swish of robes as they approached; it was like
the ominous rush of some majestic but overpowering sea. They filled the room with their
exotic strangeness. But one by one they knelt
at her feet, there in the straw, and kissed the
hem of her gown. And they gazed long upon
the baby, who smiled at them with his great
liquid eyes and strove within his bindings, as
if to reach out to them. They laughed gently,
and opening their embroidered shawls, presented their gifts—jars of precious myrrh and
frankincense, a bolt of silk shot through with
gold, a ruby in a velvet case.

"For the king," they said, rising un-
steadily and brushing at their eyes. "For the
hope of the ages. And for you, his blessed
mother . . ." One of them draped a cashmere

shawl about Mary's slight shoulders. "And you, his father . . ." A leather bag of coins was pressed into Joseph's hand. "Use it to lighten your load. For it is a heavy load you have been elected to carry, and a long journey that you will surely have to make."

"How so?" Joseph asked. "Tell us," he begged, "you who are wise. What lies ahead for the child and for us?"

The men exchanged troubled glances. The tall Persian spoke. "Make haste to leave this place. You did well to question us. There are those in the land who would come not to worship but to destroy a rival king."

"Herod?" Joseph blanched.

"Yes, Herod, the madman. Foolishly, we stopped in Jerusalem to inquire where the child might be found. The man we spoke to seemed unduly interested in this king we sought. He made us promise that when we found him we would return and tell him. Fear not—we will return to our own countries another way. But the news will spread; there will be others who will send the information to him. Take the child and go. Do not stay here another day!"

"We are leaving for Jerusalem tomorrow," Joseph said anxiously. "We must present the child at the Temple, for the day of my wife's purification is at hand. Whatever the danger involved, that must be done."

The Chaldean physician spoke up. "Go, then. Many infants are brought to the Temple every day. Herod would not think to look for him there. But do not come back to Bethlehem."

Night now, deep night, and all was still. Now and then a dog barked somewhere, a hoof stomped, a swallow went fluttering across the ceiling. Except for these sounds, the stable was silent. Yet Mary could not sleep. Careful not to disturb Joseph, she got up and stole about, doing last-minute things for the journey. Then she crept back and gazed upon the face of the slumbering child.

"Mary?" She turned, startled to see Joseph sitting up on his pallet on the floor. His eyes were large with alarm. "Is everything all right?"

"Yes. I was only looking after the baby."

He flung off the robe and began striding about, poking the fire, turning the wick of the lantern higher. "I can't sleep either. At least I didn't think I was sleeping, but I must have been because I had a dream just now. A vivid dream. An angel stood beside me and repeated the Wise Men's warning." He was breathing hard. "Mary, they were right. We will have to flee. After the presentation tomorrow we cannot come back here, or even go home to Nazareth. We must take the child and flee into Egypt."

"Egypt!"

"Yes, the land of our people's exile. We will have to wait there until it is safe to come back."

Mary stared at him as he heated milk to calm himself. "Joseph, are you sure?"

"Yes," he said grimly, and sipped the milk from the gourd. "Yes, we must do as we are told." For, sorrowing, he saw that this was the only truth now. Forces beyond themselves had brought them to this moment and would surely guide and guard them in the hours that lay ahead.

"Oh, Joseph!" She ran to him and he held her close. "Joseph, I'm afraid. I want to go home. Home to our parents and friends in Galilee. Home to our house. I want to live as other women, I want to love you as your wife and for you to love me as my husband."

He caught his breath. . . . *But know her not until she has borne this holy one . . . Until!*

It was too much, it was more than he dared contemplate right now. Yet her words gave him a source of strength and joy he would sorely need. "Hush, we must not think of such things yet. For now, for a long time, Mary, the child must be our only concern." He kissed her tenderly and stroked her hair. "We have a long journey ahead of us, as the Wise Men said. We must be thankful that they came to warn us. And their gifts—the money will help take care of us and the child. If we are driven to it, we can even sell the ruby."

"No, it belongs to him. And the precious silks and oils." She drew away, wiping her eyes. "We will put them away for him, unto the day when he shall truly be king."

"Somehow I cannot think of our son as a king," Joseph said. "At least, not a king who will mount a throne one day and rule the world." He went and stood by the child who stirred in his sleep and whimpered and slept again. "But rather as a king who will somehow change men's hearts."

Mary followed, and he saw that she was weeping. "Oh, Joseph, our poor baby! I love him so. I would almost renounce the honor of being the chosen one if only this child could be simply our child and not subject to . . . to what both of us know must surely come to him."

"Hush," he whispered. "Hush, Mary, be still." He spoke brusquely even as he soothed her, trying to deny what now for the first time he too must force himself to face. "Why, he has a glorious fate awaiting him. God's own son! I spoke wrongly a moment ago. He will be a glorious king, greater even than David, for his kingdom will be all the world."

She was staring at the baby, across whose sleeping face a shadow now hung. It was only the shadow of a wagon tongue propped against the wall, yet she saw the dark and terrible shape of it drawn across the helpless face of her little son.

"No," she said quietly, out of her private agony of knowledge. "The prophets have already spoken of his fate. He will be no earthly king. He will be a man of sorrows whom the world will despise. He will be the scapegoat driven into the wilderness to carry away the people's sins. He will bear the whole burden of their guilt upon his shoulders. He will be led up onto a hill to be slaughtered for that guilt. He will be the sacrificial lamb."

"Don't, Mary! I cannot bear it, you cannot bear it. He will not be forced to bear it. The prophets were often madmen, claiming revelations that came from the devil and not from God."

"He will be slain," she went on, as if in a daze. "They will crucify him in the manner of thieves and Zealots. That Zealot I once saw upon a cross . . . they will make him a cross and force him to carry it for the guilt of our falling apart from God. See—the shadow of that cross is upon him now."

"Stop!" For now Joseph saw it too, and the cry was wrung from his very bowels. In anger and anguish he went to the offending shaft and carried it the length of the stable and flung it into the yard. When he came back he was trembling but calm. Mary, however, was crouched beside the manger.

"Forgive me." She lifted her wet, tormented face to his. "But, oh, Joseph, the pains that I suffered to bring him forth, what will they be compared to the suffering if this thing be fulfilled?"

"Mary, Mary." He lifted her up and held her like a child. "Hush, my love, my little wife," he said. "Does not every mother who bears a son know that he must die one day?

Doesn't every man who walks this earth carry his cross with him every day?"

He turned and looked a moment at the manger. "This is our cross, Mary—yours and mine—to know that our son's hour will come, and we cannot stop it. But this is our blessing: to know that in his living and his dying he will be lifting the yoke somewhat for all men. Life with its burdens will be more tolerable. There will be hope. Not only for the freedom of Israel, our own people, but all people who are enslaved.

"And hope for the tormented spirit, Mary. To have some link, some proof that the God we worship really cares about us. Not to have to fight God any more, not to be estranged from him." Joseph's face was working, he was struggling to make it clear. "That too is suffering, perhaps the worst suffering of all. Somehow, through this child, all this will come about."

"But he is so young, so little and young!"

He lifted her chin and gazed into her stricken face. Outside a cook crowed, signaling the coming day. The darkness was lifting, the room emerging from the shadows. Through the chink above them a pink glow began to bloom. And it seemed to Joseph that he knew now why it had been his fate to love Mary—perhaps with a greater love than man has ever been asked to give a wife. For that love was akin to the love personified in the child: *Sacrifice.*

God so loved the world that he would give up his own son. And that son, that poor doomed son . . . he, too, would love the people in it so much that he would be willing to give up his life.

To suffer that others may live, as Mary had suffered in birth. To deny oneself for those who are dearer to us than life. That is the true union of those who love. And that—that in the end was what would bring man back to be united with his God.

"I love you, Mary," Joseph said. "This child is truly a child of love, sent to us because we love each other. And the home that we will make for him will be one of love. Remember how you once told me that? Our love will help us, my darling. It will enable us to grow together in courage and strength, so that we will be worthy of this great blessing that has come to us in this stable in Bethlehem. Worthy of having him entrusted to us, for even a little while."

Mary nodded, though her eyes were wet. Bending her head, she kissed Joseph's rough hand. Then she arose and set about getting the morning meal. For it was daylight now, and they had a long, long journey ahead of them.